WATER GARDENING
BASICS

Published by Dragonflyer Press
2460 North Euclid Avenue
Upland, California 91786-1199 USA

Library of Congress Cataloging in Publication Data
Uber, William C.
    Water Gardening Basics / William C. Uber. -- Upland, Calif.,
USA: Dragonflyer Press, 1988
    1. Water gardens.   I. Title.
SB423.U24 1988   635.9′674--dc19 88-160279
ISBN 0-944933-01-7 (soft) -- ISBN 0-944933-00-9 (hard)
Printed in Hong Kong

WATER GARDENING BASICS

WILLIAM C. UBER

Dragonflyer
PRESS

I would like to thank the following people for without their enthusiasm and creative talent, this book would not have been possible: Pat Woy for copy editing; Carolyn Uber for art direction; Linda Binder for the photo editing, book layout, design and production; John Carreon for the cover design and illustrations; Marcy Stark for the interior illustrations; Diane Barefoot and Theresa Wilson for the typography; and the photo contributors including Clinton Bryant; Fran Clemence; Phillip DiGiacomo of DiGiacomo, Inc., Azusa, California; Barbara Brinkerhoff of Lifescapes, Inc., Newport Beach, California; Hildegarde Mitchell, Gene Sasse, Dennis Tannen and Carolyn Uber.

William C. Uber

For what matters most, my family.

My parents, Ted and Louella Uber, who love
water gardening and shared that love
with me.

My brother Ed and sister JoAnn, who put years
of hard work and caring into the business.

My daughters, Tina and Mandi, who brighten
every day with joy, laughter and fun.

And my wife, Carolyn, whose artistic and
creative ability is displayed throughout
this book.

CONTENTS

CONTENTS

CONTENTS

CONTENTS

Charlie Mack's pond.

Photo by Dennis Tannen

CHAPTER 1

Introduction to Water Gardening

INTRODUCTION

Balboa Park, San Diego.

Photo by Carolyn Uber.

Water in the garden. It brings us refreshing coolness on the hottest summer day. It satisfies our senses with sounds that only water can make. It delights our eyes with the unsurpassed beauty of colorful water lilies, the glimmering iridescence of fish and reflections from the sky above.

Water has immense attraction to all people. For centuries Europeans have enjoyed the beauty of fountains and water gardens in their public squares and private estates. Water gardens create "natural" focal points, whether located in the home garden, shopping mall, or office building.

This book is written to fill a void in today's selection of gardening books. A few books are sprinkled here and there, covering specific areas of water gardening such as plants and Koi, but this book is written to cover all facets of decorative water gardening for homeowners as well as professional landscapers and architects.

The word "pond" conjures up different images for different people. Some envision a farm pond with a dirt bottom, fed by a creek bed and alive with ducks and frogs. Others see a mossy-covered goldfish pool in the corner of a yard. For our purposes, the word "pond" will be used in the *Webster's Dictionary* sense: "artificially enclosed body of water; a body of standing water smaller than a lake, often artificially formed." In this book you'll also find some of the newer terms - aquasphere, aquatic habitat, aquatic environment, or waterscape.

The reasons for considering a water garden are varied. Commercial landscape architects use water in their designs for effect and uniqueness. Homeowners want to exchange their rakes, lawn mowers and weedeaters for a work free garden. Others desire a pond "just like grandpa always had," yet most of us are simply looking for a garden to enjoy, a haven for relaxation.

Water gardens create natural focal points, whether in commercial or home locations. Dr. Rutten's reservoir pond, as shown here, provides the focal point on his estate. Photo by William C. Uber.

INTRODUCTION

Water ponds are natural habitats for plants, fish and snails as well as small insects, frogs and dragonflies who come by for a drink from the garden.   Photo by William C. Uber.

Mr. & Mrs. Irv McDaniel and other homeowners around the world find pleasure and satisfaction in designing, building and stocking garden ponds.   Photo by Gene Sasse.

Water does have a relaxing affect, whether it be the rhythmic waves of the ocean, a gently running brook, or the quiet beauty of a pond. While we may be unable to recreate nature with oceans and brooks, we can find pleasure in designing and building ponds.

MOTIVES

Before deciding on a water garden, consider your motives. Ask yourself the following questions:

- *Why do I want a pond?*
- *Am I trying to save work for myself?*
- *Do I want a part of nature in my own backyard?*
- *Am I looking for a fish pond? or a plant pond? a fountain or waterfall?*
- *Do I want a pond for the dog to play in?*
- *Do I want to cool off in the pond?*
- *Am I looking for a focal point in the yard or simply a subtle blend of plants and fish?*

Many people think water gardening means digging a hole, filling it in with water, plants and fish, and that's all there is to it. While it's true that established ponds require minimal work, prospective water gardeners should realize that a certain amount of responsibility goes with a pond garden.

When you build a pond, you're putting in a natural habitat, something that is "alive" and "breathing" with plants and animals. Plants live and grow in this natural habitat; natural gas exchanges are going on; birds, bugs, fish, frogs and animals come to visit and drink from your pond. In other words, you're doing more than just cementing an area in the yard and filling it with water. You are bringing nature into your surroundings.

EXPECTATIONS

Prospective water gardeners should also examine their expectations. What do you want from your pond?

Before starting construction, you should decide if you want a fish pond, a fish and plant pond, a fountain, or a waterfall. For example, a Koi pond without plants will be constructed differently than ponds containing both fish and plants.

Do you want your pond to be a focal point - something that stands out dramatically with waterfalls or spraying fountains? Or is your life hectic

and frenzied, so you're looking for a quiet haven for meditation and relaxation?

If you expect a low maintenance, relaxing environment, you'll find it in water gardening. You may wonder how water gardening can be effortless. The answer is nature. Properly planned water gardens achieve an ecological balance of water, plants, fish, and snails.

Water ponds answer a multitude of expectations, but the final decision on what you want from your water garden must come from you.

Small or large, the versatile water garden answers a multitude of expectations.   *Photo by William C. Uber.*

5

INTRODUCTION

By balancing nature and using just a little patience, water gardens are simple to build and easy to maintain. Photo by Carolyn Uber.

SELECTING A SITE

Once you've examined your motives and expectations, your next step is to consider location. Selecting a pond site involves more than deciding where it will look best. Several factors should be taken into consideration: sunlight, drainage, eaves, trees, plants, block walls, wind, and accessibility.

SUNLIGHT - Generally speaking, a garden pond with plants and fish requires six hours of sunlight. Measure off your prospective pond site with string, rope or chalk and note the amount of sun this area receives throughout the day. The more sun your water plants receive, the better and healthier they'll bloom.

Other alternatives are available for your shady areas. For example, you might consider a waterfall without fish and plants.

DRAINAGE - Good drainage is one of the keys to success in maintaining a water garden. A low spot in the yard that naturally fills with water is not necessarily the best location for your pond. These drainage areas also bring insecticides, herbicides or roof chemicals, all of which may be harmful to plants and fish. However, by cultivating the soil and using drain pipes and plants, low areas may still be used as pond sites.

EAVES, TREES, PLANTS - Ponds should be located away from the eaves of the house, overhanging trees, and dirty plants such as bamboo or pyracantha. Toxic chemicals dripping from your roof or trees are harmful to plants and fish, and dirty plants generate a dirty pond.

Good drainage is important in maintaining a water garden. By cultivating the soil, using plants and installing a drain pipe, low areas may still be used as pond sites.

BLOCK WALLS OR BARRIERS - Healthy ponds require good air circulation, so they should not be built against block walls, wall barriers or houses. Without good circulation, the air becomes stymied, causing the water to get too hot and creating improper gas exchanges.

WIND - While circulating air is a necessity, high wind locations will bring dirt, leaves, paper, and other debris into

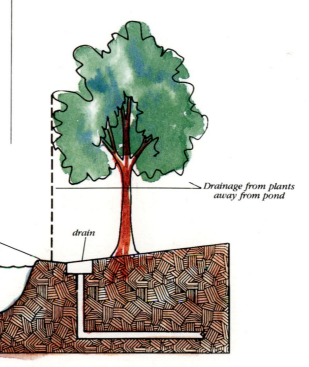

Drainage from plants away from pond

drain

Slope away from pond

INTRODUCTION

Water gardens, constructed with long-range vision and enduring qualities, offer pond owners a unique source of beauty for years to come.   Photo by William C. Uber.

(L) Picture a water garden and you probably envision the beautiful water lily.   Photo by Carolyn Uber.
(R) This office complex pond creates a natural-looking, tranquil setting.   Photo by Carolyn Uber.

your pond. Wind problems can be solved with design, skimmers, pumps, and plants, but the condition should be noted before constructing your pond.

ACCESSIBILITY - Ponds should be free and accessible from all sides, since they aren't built for wading. Water may need changing, or plants pruned, so accessibility is an important factor.

None of the above considerations are intended to frighten off the prospective water gardener. Instead, these suggestions offer pond owners the easiest, problem-free aquasphere possible. Your pond, constructed with long-range vision and enduring qualities, will be a source of beauty for years to come.

CHAPTER 2

Building Your Pond

BUILDING

Valley of the Temples. Oahu, Hawaii.

Photo by Dennis Tannen.

TYPES OF PONDS. . . FROM THE LARGE TO THE SMALL

Once you understand your motives and expectations from a water garden, and after you have carefully considered all the factors for location, you are now ready to take a closer look at the practical details of constructing your pond.

Before making all the final decisions about pond filters, skimmers, lighting, construction materials, and design, you may want to talk with a garden pond expert. These experts are not swimming pool

To make a contrast in its desert location, the Lakes Country Club in Palm Desert, California, designed 25 acres of meandering streams, shimmering lakes (shown here) and cascading waterfalls. Photo courtesy of Lifescapes, Inc.

people or a clerk at the local pet shop. They are experienced water garden consultants. (Check with your state's Association of Nurserymen or the Mail Order Association of Nurserymen for a water gardening expert in your area.) The advice offered by an expert will likely center around your answers to these and other questions:

- *What size pond do you have in mind?*
- *How many and what size fish and plants will you be stocking your pond with?*
- *Do you live in a cold or hot climate?*
- *How much daily sunlight will your pond receive?*
- *Do you live at a high altitude or a low altitude?*

The pond expert will take your answers, put them together and help you make some final decisions about your pond.

SIZE – The size of a pond should be approached with caution. There can be extremes in water gardening, from the expensive, oversized backyard pond to the limited versatility of a birdbath or tiny tub garden.

11

BUILDING

For design purposes, the size of a pond may be planned and calculated dimensionally, but for most purposes, size is discussed in gallons. For example, you may have a 4' x 10' rectangular pond that is 4' deep, but in water gardening terminology, you'll have a 1200-gallon pond. Yet, with these same dimensions, 4' x 10', but only 18-inches deep, you will only have a 450-gallon pond.

The following chart will help you calculate the surface area and the number of gallons for your prospective pond.

Gallonage is an important factor to consider when planning your pond. An overly-large pond requires the added expenses of more chemicals, filters and pumps, while the small, under 50-gallon tub garden is limited in the types and number of plants and fish it can handle. Small ponds, under 200-gallons, are also subject to temperature extremes.

Ponds within the 400-to 800-gallon size work well for beginners. They don't cost a fortune; they are easy to maintain; a variety of plants and grasses grow well; and waterfalls and fountains can be added later, if desired.

HOW TO CALCULATE POND CAPACITY

SHAPE OF POOL	FORMULA FOR GALLONS	FORMULA FOR SURFACE AREA
Rectangular or square	depth x length x width x 7.5 gallons	length x width ÷ 9 square yards of surface area
Circular	diameter x diameter x depth x 5.9 gallons	1/2 the diameter squared (times itself) x 3.14 ÷ 9 square yards of surface area
Oval	width x length x depth x 6.7 gallons	3.14 x 1/2 length x 1/2 length ÷ 9 square yards of surface area

If your location seems to command a large pond, consider grouping several smaller ponds together with a design that gives the appearance of one large pond. Then if such problems as ammonia build-up or sick fish should occur, you can easily deal with the problem on an individual pond basis.

Another method for constructing a large pond is to section the pond with one or more cement dividers, each with its own drain. Cleaning is easier and can be stretched out over a period of days by moving plants and fish to one division while cleaning the other.

In essence, the size, as well as the shape, should offer sufficient room for plants and fish, yet, allow enough water surface to capture sunlight and reflections.

SHAPE - Although your pond should be shaped and designed to fit its surroundings, it should also fit your personal desires.

The formal water garden usually calls for a square or rectangular shape, and its formality is sometimes further enhanced with the addition of statuary or fountains. Some formal ponds are built above ground, others are constructed flush against a building.

The informal yard lends itself well to an irregular shaped pond, particularly if it's located on the lawn. Circular ponds are adaptable to almost any area.

A pond shape that looks well-designed on paper may not, in fact, be your best choice. Your paper design is an aerial view, and from ground observation it may not be the most aesthetic pond. For practical viewing of your design, shape your pond with chalk, rope or a hose, stand back and study it from all angles.

DEPTH - Generally speaking, garden ponds need little more depth than 18-inches of water. A pond of this depth requires less excavating work; it has temperature stability; and it is easy to plant.

Two exceptions to the 18-inch depth are: 1) fish ponds without plants and grasses should be 3-to 4-feet deep, and 2) ponds constructed in exceptionally cold climates should be 1-foot deeper than the freezing line. Even in cold weather areas, after taking into consideration the expenses of maintaining a higher gallonage pond, it may be advisable to stay with the 18-inch depth and make a fiberglass cover or simply remove the plants for winter storage,

13

following the cold weather suggestions in Chapter Nine.

PLANNING AHEAD

Filters

The amount of filtration necessary for your pond will be in direct relationship to the pond's four basic ingredients – water lilies water grasses, fish, and snails. A well-planned water garden, using these natural ingredients has little need for filters. (See Chapter Three, "Pond Balance")

As mentioned earlier in this chapter, a water gardening expert can help you with filters. Following are four types of filters recommended for ponds with fish:

SILICA SAND FILTER - This type of filter, which has vacuuming capabilities, is excellent for large ponds, 2000-gallons or more, where the fish are well fed and there is a large amount of surface area with only a few plants. A sand filter catches heavy surface material and fish waste, turning it into backwash, which can then be used as plant or lawn fertilizer.

For ponds up to 10,000 gallons, use a 21"-diameter sand filter with a 1-hp. pump, and for 10,000 to 40,000 gallon ponds, use a 31"-diameter sand filter and a 2-hp. pump.

For ponds over 40,000 gallons, a system of tandem filters and pumps will be necessary.

ACTIVATED CHARCOAL/CARBON FILTER - Charcoal/carbon filters with zeolite added are excellent for removing algae and problem elements such as ammonia, nitrates, nitrites, and phosphates. Unless your pond has a great amount of fish waste, this type of filter is usually the best. However, charcoal filters take a small amount of maintenance since they must occasionally be removed, rinsed off, and replaced. Also, charcoal filters need reactivating. They should be allowed to dry out completely in the sun every six months. For larger ponds, two filter units may be necessary. While one unit filters the pond, the other can be reactivating. Replacement units are needed every two to three years. If desired, you can make your own charcoal unit by using one-pound charcoal with 2-ounces zeolite for 1100-gallons of water.

MICRON FILTER - Only micron-size material filters through the micron filter. This means it is effective for removing algae, but not for removing elements, compounds or chemicals. This fiberglass and plastic filter works well for ponds with fountains or statuary. It keeps the water clear and the

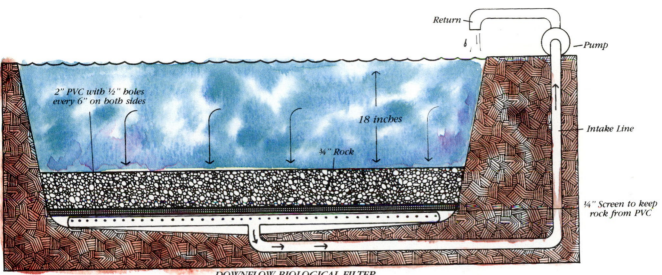

Return — Pump

Intake Line

2" PVC with ½" holes every 6" on both sides

18 inches

¾" Rock

¼" Screen to keep rock from PVC

DOWNFLOW BIOLOGICAL FILTER

This downflow biological filter uses three-quarter size rock, wire mesh and pipe to return the liquid nutrients to the pond. Eventually the pond must be emptied to remove the solid waste.

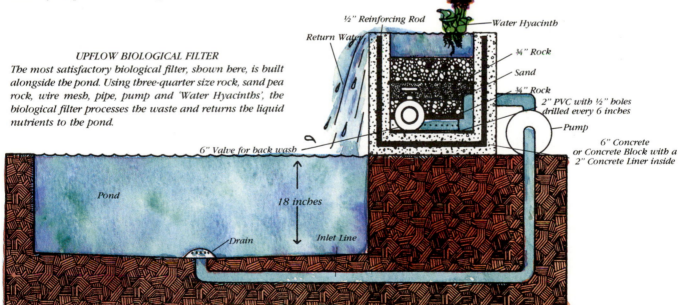

½" Reinforcing Rod — Water Hyacinth

Return Water

¾" Rock

Sand

¾" Rock

2" PVC with ½" holes drilled every 6 inches

Pump

6" Concrete or Concrete Block with a 2" Concrete Liner inside

UPFLOW BIOLOGICAL FILTER

The most satisfactory biological filter, shown here, is built alongside the pond. Using three-quarter size rock, sand pea rock, wire mesh, pipe, pump and 'Water Hyacinths', the biological filter processes the waste and returns the liquid nutrients to the pond.

6" Valve for back wash

Pond

18 inches

Drain — Inlet Line

BUILDING

lines free-flowing. Maintenance is easy – simply hose off the removable cartridge and replace.

BIOLOGICAL FILTER - This centuries old method of filtering a pond is still popular today. Although some ponds are constructed with a biological filter at the bottom, this method is generally impractical since there is no way to clean or get into the pond without disturbing the life forces.

The most satisfactory method of constructing this filter is to build another pond alongside the live pond that measures one-fourth the size. As shown in the illustrations, this filter can be built as either an upflowing or downflowing filter, using three-quarter size rock, sand, pea rock, wire mesh, pipe and a pump.

One of the most important factors to remember with a biological filter is to make sure the holes in the pipe are 1/2-inch in diameter and at least a minimum total area of 3 times the diameter of the pipe. For ponds under 5,000-gallons, use a 1-1/2 hp. pump, 5,000-25,000 gallons use a 1-1/2 hp. pump and over 25,000-gallons use a 2 hp. pump.

This filtering system should be cleaned periodically since the water going through the filter eventually begins channeling. Use a high-pressure hose nozzle to stir up the rock and sand. Green pond water usually means the filter needs cleaning.

Pumps

As in other areas of pond construction, a water gardening expert will be helpful in selecting a pump that meets your needs. You might also check the instructions included with a new pump, matching your needs with the size and type of pump. Basically, the pump should turn the water over once an hour.

SUBMERSIBLE PUMP - The simplest method of pond drainage and circulation is the submersible pump, which circulates, filters and empties the pond for cleaning. It is easy to install, quiet and economical to operate. Refer to Chapter Eight on waterfalls for more information on using a pump.

SUMP PUMP - This type of pump is usually not recommended for pond use since it uses a great deal of electricity and has no back pressure capabilities.

EXTERIOR SELF-PRIMING PUMP - This type of pump, similar to those used in swimming pools, is located outside the pond and usually set above the water level. It

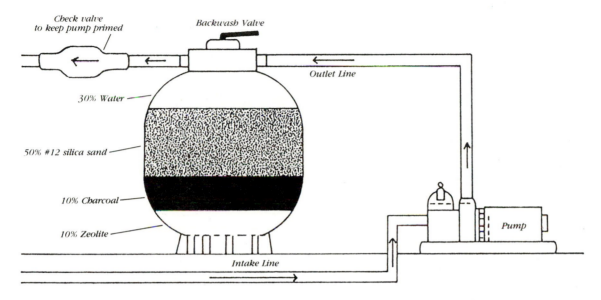

Check valve
to keep pump primed

Backwash Valve

Outlet Line

30% Water

50% #12 silica sand

10% Charcoal

10% Zeolite

Pump

Intake Line

COMMERICAL SAND FILTER
By using layers of zeolite, charcoal and sand, the sand filter catches heavy material and fish waste, turning it into backwash,
which can then be used as plant or lawn fertilizer. This type of filter is excellent for large ponds.

should be housed off the ground on a cement slab in a weatherproof chamber with 220 electrical wiring. A self-priming pump is versatile, having such capabilities as backwashing, skimming and vacuuming.

 SIPHONING - An inexpensive method of emptying the pond is siphoning. All you need are two hoses connected together and a spot lower than the pond. Start the siphon working by placing one end of the hose at the low spot on your property and begin filling this end with tap water. Once the siphon hose fills with water, remove the tap hose and let the water siphon. Be sure to put wire over the hose end that remains in the pond to prevent fish from getting caught during the siphoning process.

Skimmers

 If you are using an exterior self-priming pump with a sand filter, a skimmer is recommended. The skimmer adds two additional features: 1) It skims the surface of the pond, and 2) a vacuum line can be attached.

17

BUILDING

The placement of the skimmer is important. You can either check your yard to see where the leaves and dust settle, or check a nearby swimming pool to see where its skimmer is placed. The winds should also work with your skimmer in keeping the water surface clean.

Vacuums

All pond vacuuming supplies – flex hoses, telescopic poles, vacuum heads, hoses – are available at swimming pool supply stores. Remember to backwash after vacuuming.

Lights

Pond lighting is another factor to take into consideration before constructing your pond. Waterfalls and fountains are two water garden features that become even more dramatic at night when accented by lighting. Even if you don't plan on lights in the beginning, it might be wise to install another 1-inch line using electrical 90's to run your electrical lines through in case you change your mind later.

Exterior spotlights are the simplest and least expensive method of accenting your pond. Positioning lights on the rim of the pond, trees, walls, or eaves can add a dramatic effect to your fountain or waterfall, or they can be arranged to highlight your night-blooming water lilies.

Interior underwater lights are available in two types: swimming pool/spa lights or

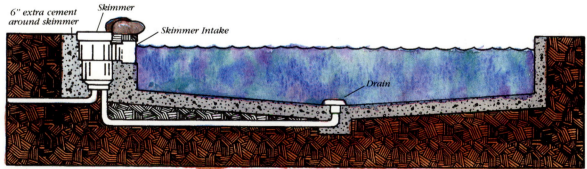

BOTTOM DRAIN WITH SKIMMER
By using a bottom drain with a skimmer, the amount of water can be regulated and a vacuum line can be attached to the skimmer.

6" extra cement around skimmer *Skimmer* *Skimmer Intake* *Drain*

specialty lights. Swimming pool/spa lights are advantageous for several reasons. They are inexpensive, easily accessible at pool supply stores, and the parts are replaceable. Only speciality pond lights are weighted and come with a flat or hinged base grate over the top.

Leave ample line within the pond when installing your underwater lights so they can be removed from the water to replace light bulbs.

Building codes usually require that the light be attached to an outside "J" box with a ground fault interrupter (GFI) and located 5-feet away from the pond. Check with your local Planning Department for other electrical regulations. You may want to hire an electrical contractor to do the installation.

In commercial ponds without plant life, lights are used to accent the pond and fish in the open areas. In order to curtail vandalism or burglary at commercial sites, 110-volt lights are available with grates over the top.

Float Valves

Float valves automatically maintain the level of water in your pond and add water as

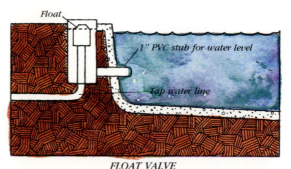

FLOAT VALVE
To maintain a certain water level, this valve will automatically release more water when the float drops down.

needed. Install the float bracket at the pond's edge and run copper tubing from the water supply to the valve. Although swimming pool suppliers stock float valves, complete with full installation instructions, the toilet type are commonly used.

POND CONSTRUCTION MATERIALS

CONCRETE - In years past, all ponds were constructed out of concrete, and many of these well-built, formal ponds have lasted for decades. However, cement ponds are difficult to remove, if necessary, and present a myriad of problems if they crack and leak. Although many people still prefer concrete, modern technology has now supplied us with simpler, easier methods of

19

BUILDING

Figure 1

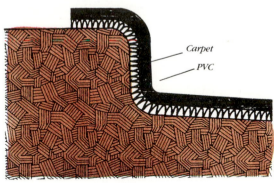

Figure 2

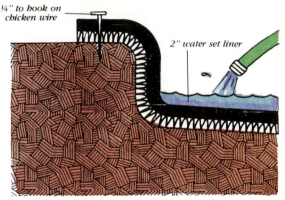

Figure 3

To protect the PVC sheeting, first line the pond with old carpet, carpet pad, builder's felt, or an old PVC liner (Figure 1). Pull the PVC sheeting over the hole as evenly as possible (Figure 2). Begin filling the pond with 2-inches of water and get into the pond to ensure that your PVC liner slides into the hole evenly. Once filled, begin making your folds and drive in a 6-inch nail every 12-inches around the perimeter (Figure 3). See page 27 for complete instructions.

constructing water gardens.

PVC - The introduction of polyvinyl chloride (PVC) sheeting has greatly improved pond building techniques. PVC is comparable in durability and length of life to concrete construction. This method of easy pond installation is highly recommended for beginners. It is inexpensive and you can start small. PVC has the necessary flexibility and stretchability that allows for water movement and ice pressure. Even if the liner should be punctured, it can be repaired easily with a patching kit.

BUTYL RUBBER - As a long-lasting synthetic, butyl rubber is more durable than PVC, but difficult to find and about twice as expensive.

POLYETHYLENE - Cheaper material than PVC, polyethylene is less flexible, has no elasticity, and breaks down quickly in sunlight.

FIBERGLASS - Maintenance-free, pre-molded fiberglass ponds are more expensive than those lined with PVC, but they will last forever. Fiberglass ponds are the easiest ponds to install. Just excavate a hole and place in the unit, refilling dirt around the edges.

ABS - Acrylonitrile butadiene styrene (ABS) plastic, pre-molded ponds are generally imported from Europe. These ponds are small, usually less than 200-gallons. These ponds should be emptied before the freezing months, since they can pop out of the ground and crack during freezing weather.

BENTONITE - As a porous clay produced by the decomposition of volcanic ash, bentonite is used mainly for large ponds, 25,000-gallons and up. Two important considerations for this type of pond are the thickness of the material and soil compaction beneath the pond. Commercial architects, or those desiring a large pond, should contact a bentonite distributor, who can help in the planning.

SOIL SEALER - If your soil contains a good proportion of clay and you are planning a lake-type pond, soil sealer may be used. The sealed pond should be excavated and compacted as suggested later in this chapter and gradually filled with water. Add soil sealer-13 (an emulsified polymer) in a 1- to 1000-parts per million proportion.

A 2% slope on the floor at one end will make emptying and cleaning easier. A 3-foot diameter bowl at the lowest point will accommodate a submersible pump for draining the pond.

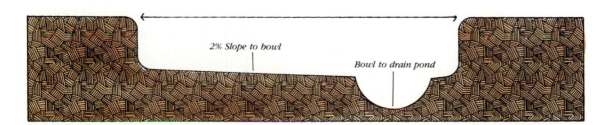

2% Slope to bowl

Bowl to drain pond

21

BUILDING

As this product seeps into the soil it creates its own liner. Since soil testing is necessary, seek an expert's advice before constructing this type of pond.

PREPARING FOR YOUR POND

Building Permits
If your pond is 18-inches or less, you probably won't need a building permit. Check with your local Planning Department for local specifications. In general, ponds should be at least 5-feet away from any structures and sources of electricity.

Electricity
You'll need to consider your source of electricity before you begin excavating. All electrical pool equipment will need grounded, three-prong outlets. Make sure pumps and underwater lights have ground fault interrupters (GFI).

Also, make certain your pond isn't located over electrical lines or water lines that may have to be moved when you begin excavating.

Excavation
LEVEL - One of the most important pre-construction factors to consider is preparing a level pond. Poorly planned ponds will end up with the water level down a few inches at one end and overflowing at the other. Using a transit level, make sure the rim of the pond is level at all sides.

Before capping the chicken wire with cement, stub-in PVC pipe for electrical lines, then bevel the sides of the pond (Figure 1). Cap the chicken wire with cement (Figure 2).

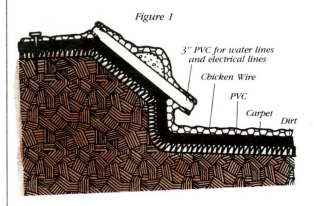

Figure 1

3" PVC for water lines and electrical lines

Chicken Wire

PVC

Carpet

Dirt

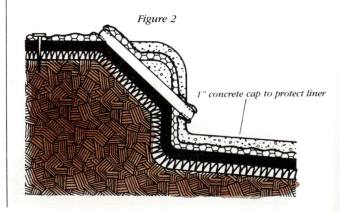

Figure 2

1" concrete cap to protect liner

(Transits can be rented from local rental yards.)

Without a transit level, an alternate method employs the use of clear tubing. Cut a length of clear tubing equal to the longest stretch of the pond, plus five feet. Since water will level in the tubing, work with a partner and watch the water level as you check the pond from all sides. A series of stakes driven into the ground at the desired level will help ensure consistency.

2% GRADE - A 2-percent slope on the pond floor at one end will make emptying and cleaning easier. At the lowest point of the 2-percent grade, dig a 1-foot deep hole, gently sloping the sides to form a 3-foot diameter bowl. This bowl will accommodate a submersible pump for draining the pond and makes washing the pond bottom easier.

DRAINS - Generally speaking, drains and overflows are unnecessary. However, a drain will simplify pond cleaning and prevent problems in the event of heavy rainfall. Place the drain in the center of the 3-foot diameter bowl. If the bottom drain will be hooked to a pump, place the overflow on a separate line. Make sure the overflow is a 2-inch size line or larger. The drain should use 2-inch line for ponds under 5,000 gallons, and 3-inch line up to 50,000 gallons. Since commercial ponds are subject to more debris, use 3-inch for under 5,000 and 5-inch up to 50,000.

BUILDING THE CEMENT POND

Preparing the Pipe Lines

After excavating, following the above instructions on leveling, sloping, and draining, now is the time to install the skimmer and electrical lines. Even if you opt not to use a drain or pump at this time, it may be wise to go ahead and stub-in two 2-inch lines, placing one in the drain hole, and the other at the opposite side of the pond on the bottom or on the side near the bottom in the event you decide to install them at a later date. Remove the dirt around the stubbed-in pipes to allow at least 6-inches of cement around the pipe for greater protection from cracking. All pipes below the pond must be covered with 2-inches of dirt before cementing except in cases where they extend through the cement. Cap all the stubs before cementing the pond. If the pipes are not going to be hooked to a pump,

BUILDING

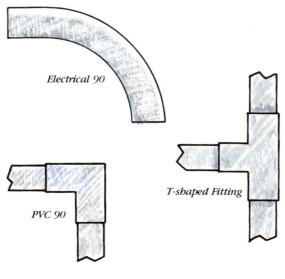

Electrical 90

T-shaped Fitting

PVC 90

PLUMBING FITTINGS

they need not be pressurized. However, if they are going to be hooked to a self-priming pump system, they must be glued and pressurized to 40 lbs. pressure, holding for 15 minutes, to ensure that there are no leaks. (Pressure valves and garden hose adapters may be purchased at your local swimming pool supplier.) In order to prevent back pressure and clogging, use electrical 90's or 30-degree 90's instead of the standard 90.

Preparation for Cement

The dirt area for the pond must be level, smooth and hard packed. (Keep in mind that the excavated site should be larger than the finished pond by the thickness of the cement.) If you had to refill an area, tamp thoroughly and use a sprinkler overnight to pack the soil. Care should be taken not to undermine the area by overwatering.

Begin construction by installing 1/2-inch rebar every 12-inches on center, tying for structure. Raise the rebar 2-inches above the soil line (special bricks are available for raising rebars), so that the cement will totally surround the rebar. Lay chicken wire on top of the rebar. For ponds over 50,000 gallons, use 3/4-inch rebar and #3 construction wire on top. (Note: Double check to make sure all pipes are covered with 2-inches of soil except where they extend through the cement.)

SUBMERSIBLE PUMP - If you are using a submersible pump in the pond, run a 2- or 3-inch PVC line from 5- to 10-inches below the water level straight out, using electrical 90's, extending above the water level out to the waterfall area or electrical supply line. Two- to three-inch pipes are large enough for the water lines and the electrical lines to go through without laying them over the sides. The plugs should never be cut on submersible pumps. Run the entire line and plug through the PVC pipe. The PVC pipe must come up above the water level outside the pond.

Cement for the Pond

If you are purchasing your concrete, ask for the water-tight mix. If you are mixing your own cement, the most common mix is:

- *1 shovel plastic cement*
- *3 shovels sand*
- *Soil dye, if desired, to your specifications.* (Colors: black, adobe, green, blue and white.)

In areas of heavy freezing or land movement, 5- to 8-inches of cement will be necessary. Four inches is the minimum.

PVC pipes which extend through the cement remain unobtrusive when the pond is finished off with rocks, flagstone or bricks, for example.

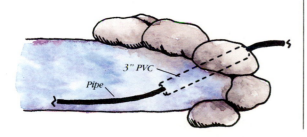

ROCKS - Since rocks can weaken the cement mix, they are not recommended. Also, don't lay cement around rocks as part of your pond. These rocks have a different expansion and contraction ratio, and eventually may lead to cracking. The entire pond must be laid before adding such features as rocks, wood, or lava. The only things extending through the cement are the PVC pipes.

DYE - Soil-colored dye is readily obtained at most hardware stores. Be consistent in the measurement of your dye to maintain uniformity in color. Remember, the darker the color the more you enhance the color of your fish and plants.

WATERFALL - At this point, you may want open areas for laying a waterfall line. Beginners should consider adding a waterfall at a later date, following the instructions in Chapter Eight.

Forming the Pond

The pond must be cemented all at once, keeping the mixture as dry and consistent as possible. Concrete batches mixed on different days have different expansion and contraction ratios. Since concrete must be poured all at once, you will probably have to

BUILDING

form the sides with 2 x 6's, 3/4 plywood sheets, or reinforced bender board. (Bender board may be used but will need heavy support.) To go around gentle corners, take a skill saw and cut the plywood 3/4's of the way through, about every 1/4-inch. Then wet the plywood and flex as needed. Add more cuts if necessary. Remove the forms approximately 2 hours after setting or when hardened, and patch any holes left by the forms. Keep the cement moist by sprinkling with a fine mist as needed. Never allow the cement to dry out.

Gunite/Plaster Ponds

Instead of using concrete, many large ponds are sprayed under pressure with Gunite, covered with plaster, and finished off with decorative tile around the water line. Since the Gunite mixture is not watertight, a covering of plaster is a necessity. Unfortunately, if plaster dries out, it cracks, so this type of pond requires moisture at all times, making pond cleaning a difficult procedure.

Constructing a divided pool, as mentioned earlier under "Pond Size," is the most logical answer for solving pond cleaning problems with Gunite/Plaster construction.

Curing the Pond

Cement should harden approximately eight hours and be kept moist at all times. Although too much water will weaken the cement, it should be misted periodically. After about eight hours, when the cement is hard, fill the pond with water.

Following are two methods of curing the cement pond:

#1 - Fill the pond with water, and mix one gallon of inexpensive vinegar to every 200-gallons of pond water. Let it stand for five days, then drain, rinse and fill immediately, without allowing the pond to dry out.

#2 - Purchase a gallon of muriatic acid at your local pool supply company, and mix with four gallons of water. Using a broom, brush the solution over all the cemented area of your pond. Immediately rinse and fill the pond. (Note: Muriatic acid can burn skin, eyes and clothing. Use with caution. Safety glasses and a pollen filter mask are recommended.)

After curing, fill the pond with fresh water and follow the instructions in Chapter Three under "Preparing the Newly-Constructed Pond."

BUILDING

NEVER LET A CEMENT POND DRY OUT. Once a cement pond has been formed and set, it starts a 99-year hardening process under water. If at any time you allow the pond to dry out, the cement will shrink and crack. Using cement dyes eliminates the necessity of painting, thereby preventing the pond from drying out and possibly cracking.

BUILDING THE PVC LINER POND

After excavating, following the earlier instructions on leveling and sloping, you are now ready to prepare for the PVC liner. For a long-lasting pond, most experts recommend using 12 mil. PVC or heavier.

To determine the size of liner you need, add the maximum width of the pond once, plus depth twice, plus two feet for a 12-inch overlap on each side. Repeat for length.

For a 13' x 13' x 18" deep pond, you will need the following materials:

- *18' x 18' lining material (carpet, felt, tarpaper, etc.)*
- *18' x 18' PVC Sheeting (12 mil. or fish quality)*
- *18' x 48' chicken wire*
- *Ready-mix cement/ or mix your own*
- *20-30 bricks or rocks for weights*
- *56 6-inch nails*

The dirt area for the pond must be smooth, level, and hard packed. Compaction is an important factor in the construction of PVC ponds. If any of the area was refilled, tamp thoroughly. Use a sprinkler overnight to pack the soil, taking care not to undermine the area by overwatering.

To protect the PVC sheeting, line the pond area with old carpet, carpet pad, builder's felt, or an old PVC liner. Cut and trim the protective liner to fit the hole. Do not attach the protective liner in place with nails, wire or anything that might puncture the PVC sheeting.

For easier installation, lay the PVC sheeting in the sun to warm. Pull the sheeting over the hole as evenly as possible. Place a hose in the center of the sheeting and fill with 2-inches of water. As the pond fills, the sheeting will slide into the hole. Roll up your pants and get inside the pond to ensure that your liner slides into the hole evenly without obstruction. Bricks or rocks placed

27

around the edge of the pond as weights will hold the sides until they can be secured.

Once the pond is filled with 2-inches of water, you are ready to fold and secure the sides. A few folds or wrinkles in the PVC allow the pond to move, float, expand, and contract, especially in areas with high land movement or cold climate areas. Pinch a 1- to 2-inch fold at the bottom of each side to allow for pond movement. Now, take the sides of the sheeting and begin making a series of neat folds, all facing one direction, in those places where the sheeting begins to bunch up. At the top of the liner, go back 4-inches from the top edge of the pond and drive in a 6-inch nail every 12-inches around the perimeter as you fold and set the sides. While working, make sure the fold is in place at the bottom of the sides. Leave 1/2-inch of the nail exposed for attaching the chicken wire. Make sure all the nails are 4-inches back from the edge of the pond. If they are below water level, your PVC liner will not hold water.

WATERFALL - At this point, you may want to leave an area open for laying a waterfall line, making sure to install a 2- to 3-inch pipe at an angle for electrical and water lines. Beginners should consider adding a waterfall at a later date, following the instructions in Chapter Eight.

Chicken Wire
Remove water from the pond with a submersible pump, by siphoning downhill, or by bailing out.

If your pond is approximately 18-inches deep, buy 24-inch chicken wire. Run the chicken wire around the perimeter of the pond, attaching one side to the nails which are extended above the liner. The other end of the chicken wire should just touch the bottom of the pond. Take care not to puncture the sheeting by bending the sharp ends of the chicken wire away from the PVC liner. Gently fold and press the chicken wire to lay flat on top of the liner. The chicken wire is a structure for the cement. Lay chicken wire over the bottom if it is also going to be cemented.

Cement
The type of cement isn't important since it need not hold water; however, a plastic cement is easy to work with. Cement for a PVC-lined pond is merely a capping to protect the liner from weather, hydro-carbons, animals, and to make the pond visually pleasing. Cracks are not a factor

when the pond is PVC lined.

Mix your cement, using sand or soil and cement. Following is a common mix:

- *1 shovel cement*
- *4 shovels sand or soil*
- *1/2 gallon fire clay for every 15 shovels of mix*
- *Soil dye, if desired*

Fire clay, available at most hardware stores, makes the cement gummy and easier to handle. Dye, which gives the cement a soil look, may also be obtained from the hardware store. For uniformity in color, be consistent in the measurement of the dye.

The best method for cementing the sides is to work on a 10-foot long 6-inch high area. Cement two of these lengths, then return to the first length and add another 6-inches in height. This method allows the lower cement to harden and structure enough to hold the second and third 6-inch sections. About 1/2-inch of cement is needed to cover the chicken wire.

Wait two or three days after the cement has hardened before trimming off the excess liner. Do not lay cement out to the dirt or you may get a capillary action of water out of the pond.

Finishing Treatment

In order to protect the PVC liner from deteriorating in the sun and air, it is important to cap off the pond. The slurry that forms at the bottom as the water drains out of the cement makes a good base for your top cap. Although cement is the most common method for concealing the edge of the PVC liner, the choice of the final appearance should reflect your personal taste and landscaping decor. There are several ways to finish and blend your pond into the landscaping, such as using bricks, cement blocks, stone, flagstone, wood, railroad ties without creosote, and turf, all the end result of making certain the PVC liner is completely covered. Note: Make sure the capping-off product does not contain any toxic substances.

Since a rough texture is preferable on a pond both for looks and safety, use old canvas gloves to pat the cement onto the chicken wire. A rough textures helps to prevent you from slipping when you are cleaning the pond. If the glove texture isn't appealing, try using a brush.

Curing

For curing, allow the cement to set for about

eight hours, keeping it moist at all times with a light misting. (Do not use acid on PVC liner ponds). Before filling the pond with water, fill a hose sprayer with liquid detergent. Spray the pond down with this soapy solution, then rinse thoroughly with fresh water. Pump the water out and rinse again with fresh water.

After rinsing the pond, fill with fresh water and follow the instructions in Chapter Three under "Preparing Your Newly-Constructed Pond."

INSTALLING THE FIBERGLASS POND

Although more expensive than other types but less than cement, fiberglass ponds are the simplest to install since they come in solid, pre-formed modular units. The pre-drilled modular units can be attached together with silicon and stainless steel nuts and bolts. PVC compression fittings for pumps, filters or drainage systems are installed by cutting a hole in the fiberglass with a sabre saw or portable drill with a hole saw. Use silicone rubber as a sealant.

Fiberglass ponds should be cleaned before using to remove any residual toxic materials or chemicals. Fill a hose sprayer with liquid detergent, spray the pond down with this soapy solution, then rinse thoroughly with fresh water.

Although these tough, indestructible units can withstand temperatures as low as 30 degrees below, weather is a factor when cleaning the pond. Fiberglass ponds should be cleaned during dry weather, since they may pop out of the ground if emptied and cleaned during wet weather.

Leveling, following the earlier instructions in this chapter, is important when installing fiberglass ponds. Also, once the unit is in place, fill immediately with water to weight the pond. Mix the extra soil with plenty of water and tamp the mixture into the crevices for a solid, tight fit in the ground.

A variety of pond creations can be achieved by using any combination of shapes and sizes.

PAINTING THE POND

Before filling your newly-constructed cement or fiberglass pond with water, you may wish to enhance its overall appearance with paint. Dark colors, such as deep green or blue, brown, or black, are best. Not only do these deep colors give a cleaner appearance to a live pond, but they enhance the colors of your fish and flowers.

In order for paint to penetrate the surface of a cement pond, you'll need to etch the pond. The quickest and easiest method is to mix 1-gallon of muriatic acid with 4-gallons of water and brush the solution over all the cemented area. (Wear safety glasses and a pollen mask when working with muriatic acid.) Immediately rinse thoroughly and allow it to dry completely before painting. Use a rubber-based paint on cement ponds.

Before painting fiberglass, acetone the entire surface to remove all wax. Use an epoxy paint on fiberglass.

Although the cement capping can be dyed or painted, PVC sheeting cannot be painted.

REPAIRING THE DAMAGED POND

Just as your house or your car may need occasional repairing, likewise your pond may suffer damage in one way or another.

ROOT DAMAGE - Unfortunately, tree roots continually seek the nourishment of pond water, particularly if your pond has a leak, and represent an ongoing problem unless the tree and its troublesome roots are removed. Once the roots have been removed, empty the pond and reseal the damaged area by lining with PVC sheeting, which has been nailed to the sides, and cover with 1/2-inch of cement.

ANIMAL DAMAGE - Although fiberglass and concrete can withstand animals in the pond, PVC and butyl rubber can be punctured by an animal's nails. Empty the pond and re-seal the damaged area using a PVC patch kit and hair dryer to dry and seal the new patch.

SUN & HYDROCARBON DAMAGE - Eventually, excessive sun damage and hydrocarbons will affect all types of ponds, from PVC to cement, although fiberglass best withstands the ravages of the sun. The best protection for PVC is to properly cap the pond off with cement and always keep the pond filled with water. Once a PVC pond begins to crack from this type of damage, the liner usually has to be replaced.

EARTHQUAKES/LAND MOVEMENT - Land movement also causes problems with all types of ponds, and is a strong factor for

BUILDING

consideration before installing a pond. Each type of pond requires its own installation techniques to keep damage to a minimum. Fiberglass ponds should be placed in soft soil to allow for land movement; PVC ponds should be pinched in an inch or so at the bottom when being installed, allowing it to move and float during earth movement; and cement ponds need heavily-packed soil for structural support. For repair, fiberglass may be reglassed and PVC and cement ponds may be re-lined with PVC.

WEIGHT - Few people take into consideration the weight of water when constructing a pond, and therefore are tempted to skimp on construction requirements. Water weighs eight pounds per cubic foot. Couple that weight with water movement, which is naturally created by land movement and temperature changes, and you'll understand how weight can eventually tear up a pond. The better the construction, the longer the pond will last.

CEMENT CRACKS - Painting is used on old, porous cement ponds. If you detect a crack, you can either drain the pond and repair, or you can use a pond patch that sets up under water. In areas with continual expansion and contraction use silicone or tar, although as a temporary measure, it only lasts from 6 to 24 months.

CHAPTER 3

Pond Balance

POND BALANCE

Japanese Garden, Cal-State Long Beach.

Photo by Carolyn Uber.

NATURE AND WATER WORKING TOGETHER

Novices to the world of water gardening may wonder why so much emphasis is placed on pond balancing. After all, once you've finished building your pond it's simple – just add some dechlorinator to the water, plant a few water lilies, stock with a few fish and sit back and relax; then if the water turns green with algae, just empty it and start over again. . . and start over again. . . and start over again.

Let's take a closer look at the natural processes a pond goes through. In constructing and stocking the pond, everything was rushed at dizzying speed compared to the slow way Nature would have gone about it. All the pond components - water, fish, plants, snails, soil, and pond construction materials - have been suddenly combined without time to adjust and interact. Within a few days of filling, the pond water starts turning murky, taking on a green or brown tinge. Left unchecked, this will often progress to thick "pea soup" water. What has happened?

Your pond has algae, a condition that is both inevitable and natural. The only problem is in *how* you handle the situation, and starting over by adding fresh water is not the way to balance a pond.

Clear Water Formula

The best way to prevent excessive algae is through balancing the pond's components. Although each pond differs in the amount of sun, depth, dimensions, water movement, and temperatures, the following clear water formula should help you in achieving pond balance. For each *square yard* of *surface area*, you should have:

- *Two bunches oxygenating grasses*
- *One medium to large water lily*
- *Twelve water snails*
- *Two fish, 4" to 5"*

With proper planning of all its components -- water, fish, plants, snails, soil, and pond construction materials -- each pond goes through a natural balancing process.

POND BALANCE

OXYGENATING GRASSES - The oxygenating grasses are important. They replenish evaporating oxygen through the process known as photosynthesis. Carbon dioxide is drawn in at night and oxygen given off during sunlight. Oxygenating plants absorb carbon dioxide, caused by wastes from animal life and decaying matter, and convert it into carbohydrates, which are needed for plant growth. At the same time, they release oxygen into the water, which is essential to the balance of the pond. You can often see tiny bubbles of oxygen rising to the surface from these plants.

By covering the water surface with its leaves, 'Attraction' and all water lilies play a role in pond balancing. Photo by Carolyn Uber.

WATER LILIES - Water lilies also play a part in pond balance. They keep the pond from losing its oxygen and taking in too much carbon dioxide by covering the water surface with their leaves. Water lilies keep the pond from breathing too fast. Through the photosynthesis process, a body of water breathes much like people do. From about 1:00 a.m. until around 9:00 a.m., your pond takes in carbon dioxide for the plants, then during the day from about 10:00 a.m. until about 6:00 p.m., your pond gives off oxygen. In other words, as the temperature warms, so does the breathing in your pond.

During the cooler winter months, when the growing and breathing process slows down, you will notice your pond clearing. Then in the summer the pond will turn green again as the breathing process increases before the plants have grown large enough to offer surface protection.

Too much coverage is as bad as too little coverage. During the winter your pond requires very little coverage of water lily leaves. But during the summer your pond should have 60- to 70-percent coverage. More than 75-percent will hinder the pond.

FISH - Fish are the pond's gardeners. They eat the excess plant material, algae, and pests. In a balanced pond, fish are never fed by the gardener.

SNAILS - Snails perform the important function of consuming algae. They keep the plants from being choked out by eating algae off the plants and pots.

Any changes made in the basic clear water formula must be compensated for in one way or another, whether by changing the proportion of plant material, adding algaecides, or adding pond filtration. For example, if you decide to add bog plants, then reduce the number of water lilies proportionately up to 20-percent. For each 10 water lilies, eliminate no more than 20-percent or two water lilies for two bog plants. With small flowering aquatics, reduce the number of water lilies by 1/6th. Also, if your pond is deeper than 18-inches, increase the amount of oxygenating grasses by two bunches for each additional 6-inches of depth.

The length of time for pond balancing depends on such variables as weather, water chemistry, the number of fish, the number of plants, and the richness of the soil.

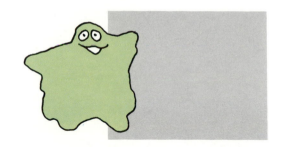

ALGAE IS YOUR FRIEND

Don't become alarmed at the sight of green water (algae) in your pond. Algae, simple forms of plant life, naturally occur wherever water and light exist. Instead of considering algae as a pond problem, you can learn to recognize and appreciate your algae as a friend – a friend who's telling you what is happening in your pond.

Ponds containing natural life are not intended to be crystal clear like swimming pools. Once your oxygenating grasses and water lilies become established, the water will begin clearing, even overnight in some cases. As long as your pond is properly balanced and the bottom waste removed monthly or quarterly, it will never become stagnant.

Whatever you do, don't change the pond water. You will only start the "balancing" process all over again. After the

Above: The aquatic plants in the water garden at Workman Park, City of Industry, California, add special dimensions to the pond -- beauty and life.   Photo by Gene Sasse. Left: A wooden dock at the Nash home raises several inches over their lily-filled pond.   Photo by Carolyn Uber.

Opposite - Clockwise from Top Left: By planting various types of aquatics, the Workman Park water garden takes on its own unique appearance. Photo by William C. Uber.; A beautiful 'Yellow Dazzler' water lily comes under close scrutiny by the pond's resident bullfrog. Photo by William C. Uber.; The pond at the Prudential Building, Canoga Park, California beautifully reflects the building and overhead clouds. Photo by Gene Sasse.; Every pond has its own characteristics and personality.   Photo by Carolyn Uber.

POND BALANCE

first weeks, most ponds remain balanced for years. A little patience goes a long way!

Your newly-established pond will begin developing a hard biological waste center on the bottom of the pond. This sewer, which includes fish droppings, dead leaves, dirt and waste from the air, is broken down in the water and offers nutrients for the plants.

To be healthy all ponds need a certain amount of bottom waste. If the bottom waste, particularly in the fall and winter, is so rich that the grasses and water lilies cannot consume it fast enough, then algae will result. Monthly vacuuming of about 70-percent of the bottom material is the usual formula. Vacuuming more often only disturbs your pond unnecessarily.

Types of Algae

There are hundreds of colors and types of algae. The invisible spores that start algae are borne by the wind. The color depends on its geographic region. Soil or water alkalinity/acidity and temperatures play their parts in the color of the algae.

For general discussion, algae can be divided into three categories: free-floating algae (green water), hair algae, and green slime.

FREE-FLOATING ALGAE - This green water algae is prevalent during the first 90 days of pond balancing, or on occasions when the weather suddenly turns warm. Free-floating algae signifies a gas problem, a low oxygen/high carbon dioxide problem, or a high nutrient content in the pond's water.

Green water is Nature's way of balancing the pond in the beginning. If the green water doesn't clear up after 60 to 90 days, you may need to take a closer look at the pond components and make some of the following changes to achieve pond balance:

- *Too many fish/overfeeding fish.*
- *Insufficient oxygenating grasses or water lily foliage.*
- *Excessive debris such as fallen leaves in the pond. (Plastic netting over the pond works well if you have a problem with falling leaves.)*
- *Lawn fertilizer has gotten into the pond. Even a few drops will cause a high nutrient content in the pond.*
- *A constant agitation of the water by large fish, fountains, or waterfalls that disturbs the natural biological sewer at the bottom of the pond.*

40

HAIR ALGAE - This type of algae forms in all types of ponds, even in balanced, clear ponds. It is recognizable as big clumps of long, stringy algae. Too many nutrients in your pond result in the formation of hair algae. The most probably source of excess nutrients are fish food, a build up of dead leaves or plant material on the bottom of the pond, and fertilizer or dirt drainage into the pond. This type of algae is highly prevalent in the spring following the fall and winter months.

The easiest method of controlling hair algae is to physically remove it from the pond. In order to prevent hair algae, you should occasionally vacuum the bottom of the pond, watch the amount of food you're feeding the fish, and remove any fallen leaves from the pond's surface.

GREEN SLIME - You'll recognize this familiar green growth that's found on the sides of ponds, troughs, or barrels, for example. This form of algae is one of the pond's stablizing forces, and your pond will not be healthy until a good layer of slime develops. Slime produces 60-percent of the oxygen in the pond. If you scrub down this slime, you'll be taking away a stabilizing life force.

Chemical Control

Chemical control, particularly as new plants are becoming established, may also be used to control algae. However, great care should be taken to select chemicals that will not harm the fish or plants. Algaecides may temporarily take care of the problem, but they're not the final answer. Whatever the source of the problem, whether insufficient plants or an overabundance of fish, you must deal with the problem of algae.

The best advice is to use no more chemicals than necessary and discontinue them as quickly as possible. Once your sophisticated pond plants take over, you'll have a natural, ecologically-balanced pond in no time.

If you choose to use chemicals, buy only clearly-labeled products that have complete instructions for pond use. Some of these products include:

POTASSIUM-BASED PRODUCT - As a pond setup algaecide, this product helps control green water and will not harm your fish or water plants when used as directed.

COPPER-BASED PRODUCT - This pond setup algaecide is effective in treating filamentous types of algae and will not harm fish or plants when used as directed.

WIDELEAF SYSTEMIC PRODUCT (Herbicide) - This algaecide is *only* recommended for established ponds or ponds without plants.

BUFFERING AGENT - This product removes nutrients, chlorine, and chemicals, starts algae control, prevents soil packing, and deodorizes the pond. It is not recommended for ponds constructed with soil sealer.

PREPARING YOUR NEWLY-CONSTRUCTED POND

After you've cured your pond, following the instructions in Chapter Two, it is time to fill the pond with fresh water and add the setup chemicals. Initially, fresh water is necessary to control the algae and to quickly establish pond balance. Water that's not fresh may contain fully-developed algae spores and with the addition of dirt planters may develop algae before the water plants have a chance to get started.

CHLORINE/CHLORAMINES - While chlorination was the predominant form of water disinfection for many years, recently many water districts/companies have switched to chloramine disinfection. Chloramine, a combination of chlorine and ammonia, is highly toxic to fish and plants at the levels being used to disinfect drinking water. Consult with someone in your water district to determine whether chloramines are being used in your water.

Chloramine and chlorine test kits, available from water garden suppliers, will enable you to determine the levels of chlorine and ammonia in your water. Several products are currently available through water garden suppliers that will remove chlorine, chloramines and ammonia from the water. These products include:

VITAMIN-BASED PRODUCT - Removes chlorine, adds a protective slime that coats the fish, and detoxifies heavy metals.

(L) The 650-year-old water garden at Ushimado Temple, Japan, enhances the beauty of the landscape design. Photo by Carolyn Uber.
(R) Visitors to Cal-State Long Beach are always attracted to the water gardens gracing the campus. Photo by Carolyn Uber.

ZEOLITE - Removes the ammonia from the chloramine, leaving the free chlorine to dissipate. In chloramine areas, use 1-lb. of zeolite in the filter per 100-gallons of pond water every six months. Without a filter, place the zeolite in the area that is in closest contact with incoming tap water.

CHLORAMINE REMOVER - This liquid ammonia and chloramine remover is frequently used with a vitamin-based product. It is harmless to plants, fish and invertebrates.

The addition of up to 5-percent fresh water at any one time does not harm the fish or plants. In fact, it appears to have value as a fungicide and algaecide. An automatic valve float is an effective way of adding water slowly on a regular basis, or an overhead lawn sprinkler used ten minutes nightly will work sufficiently.

Peaceful, relaxing water gardens were one of the major features in the design of this Orange County, California, condominium complex. *Photo by Carolyn Uber.*

60-DAY SET-UP SCHEDULES

The following maintenance schedules will help you achieve a natural balance and ultimately clear water in your new pond or newly cleaned pond quickly and efficiently.

For ponds under 1000-gallons, the potassium-based product set-up is usually recommended. While the potassium is more expensive than the copper-based product, it works quicker in cleaning the water.

Pond Set-Up Using a Potassium-Based Product

DAY 1: (Plants and fish are added on this day.)

A. Use 2 oz. chloramine remover per 100-gallons of pond water.

B. Float fish and snails for 30 minutes, following instructions in Chapter Six, then release them into the water.

C. Add 1/2 pound of buffering agent per 100 gallons of pond water.

D. Add 1/4 pound salts, using formulated fish salts or salts with anti-bacterial agents, per 100 gallons of pond water.

E. Add 2 ounces vitamin-based product per 100 gallons of pond water.

F. Plant and install the recommended numbers of oxygenating grasses, water lilies, bog plants, and ornamental grasses.

DAY 5:

A. Add 1/2 pound of buffering agent per 100 gallons of water.

B. Add 1/4 pound salts per 100 gallons pond water.

DAY 12: Add 1/2-teaspoon potassium-based product for each 100 gallons of pond water to a quart of water and mix thoroughly until crystals are dissolved. Distribute evenly in the pond water after 6:00 p.m., using a one-quart hand sprayer, taking care not to spray the solution on the plant foliage.

DAY 15: Feed fish as much as they will eat in 10 minutes, approximately one tablet per fish. NOTE: Overfeeding fish adds excess nitrogenous wastes to pond, fertilizes the algae and endangers the health of your fish.

DAY 19:

A. Repeat DAY 12 Potassium Treatment.

B. Inspect containers to ensure that plants are still properly planted.

DAY 22: Feed fish as directed on Day 15.

DAY 26: Repeat Potassium treatment.

DAY 29: Feed fish as before.

DAY 33: Repeat Potassium treatment.

DAY 36: Feed fish as before.

DAY 40: Remove cap from the Potassium-based product and place it 10-inches below the pond water surface. If the cap is clearly visible, repeat the potassium treatment and continue with the schedule. If the view of the cap is clouded, return to Day 1 and start again, omitting the salt, chloramine remover and vitamin-based product.

DAY 43: Feed fish as before.

DAY 47: Repeat Potassium treatment.

DAY 50: Feed fish as before.

DAY 54: Repeat Potassium treatment.

DAY 57: Feed fish as before.

DAY 61: Repeat Potassium treatment.

At this time your pond will begin self-balancing. Continue the chemical treatments as needed, at least once a month. Avoid the temptation to overfeed your fish. If the pond water is not clear, check the oxygenating grasses, replacing or replanting as needed. (Refer to the section "Clear Water Formula" at the beginning of this chapter.)

**Pond Set-Up Using a
Copper-Based Product**

Copper sulfate needs a catalyst in order to work. Check with your water gardening supplier for a catalyst.

DAY 1: (Plants and fish are added.)

A. Use 2 oz. chloramine remover per 100 gallons of pond water.

B. Float fish and snails for 30 minutes, following instructions in Chapter Six, then release them into the water.

C. Add 1/2 pound of buffering agent per 100 gallons of pond water.

D. Add 1/4 pound salts, using formulated fish salts or salts with anti-bacterial agents, per 100 gallons of pond water.

E. Add 2 ounces vitamin-based product per 100 gallons of pond water.

F. Plant and install the recommended numbers of oxygenating grasses, water lilies, bog plants, and ornamental grasses.

DAY 5:

A. Add 1/2 pound buffering agent per 100 gallons of pond water.

B. Add 1/4 pound salts per 100 gallons of pond water.

POND BALANCE

Orange County condominium complex.

Photo by William C. Uber.

During the summer months, ponds only need 60 to 70 percent coverage of water lily leaves.   *Photo by William C. Uber.*

DAY 10: Mix 1/8-teaspoon copper-based product per 100 gallons of pond water in one-quart water. Mix well and spray solution on 1/2 of the pond's surface, taking care not to spray plant foliage.

DAY 11: Repeat copper treatment on second half of the pond's surface.

DAY 12: Repeat copper treatment on first half of the pond's surface.

DAY 14: Repeat copper treatment on second half of the pond's surface.

DAY 15: Repeat copper treatment on second half of the pond's surface.

DAY 17: Feed fish as much as they will eat in 10 minutes, approximately one tablet per fish. NOTE: Overfeeding fish adds excess nitrogenous wastes to pond, fertilizes algae and endangers the health of your fish.

DAY 20:

A.   Repeat copper treatment on first half of pond's surface, increasing dosage to 3/8-teaspoon per 100 gallons of pond water.

B: Inspect containers to ensure plants are still planted properly.

DAY 24: Feed fish as before.

DAY 27: Repeat copper treatment on second half of pond's surface, using 3/8-teaspoon per 100 gallons of pond water.

DAY 31: Feed fish as before.

DAY 34: Repeat copper treatment on first half of pond's surface, using the 3/8-teaspoon per 100 gallons of water.

DAY 38: Feed fish as before.

DAY 41: Remove cap from copper-based product and place it 10-inches below the pond water surface. If the cap is clearly visible, continue the copper treatments, using 3/8-teaspoon per 100 gallons of pond water on the second half of the pond's surface. Continue with the treatment schedule. If the view of the cap is clouded, return to Day 1 and start again, omitting the salt, vitamin-based product and chloramine remover.

47

POND BALANCE

DAY 45: Feed fish as before.

DAY 47: Repeat copper treatment, using 3/8-teaspoon per 100 gallons of pond water, spraying first half of pond's surface.

DAY 52: Feed fish as before.

DAY 54: Repeat copper treatment, using 3/8-teaspoon per 100 gallons of pond water, spraying second half of the pond's surface.

DAY 59: Feed fish as before.

At this time the pond will start self-balancing. Continue the chemical treatments as needed, at least once a month. Avoid the temptation to overfeed your fish. If the pond water is not clear, check the oxygenating grasses, replacing or replanting as needed. (Refer to the section "Clear Water Formula" at the beginning of this chapter.)

Each pond will vary in the amount of sun, depth, dimensions, water movement and temperature. Yet, balancing can be achieved with the "Clear Water" formula using fish, oxygenating grasses, water snails and water lilies as noted in this chapter.

CHAPTER 4

Aquatic Plants

AQUATIC PLANTS

Workman Park, City of Industry.   *Photo by William C. Uber.*

No true garden pond is complete without aquatic plants. Those ponds without plants are simply reflection ponds or fish ponds. Chapter Three noted the ecological role of aquatic plants in the garden pond, but plants add even further dimensions – beauty and life.

Selecting aquatic plants will be no easy chore since there is a wide variety of aquatic plants, from tiny duckweed to the amazing *Victoria amazonica,* the oversized queen of all water lilies.

The delicate cascade of pale lavender petals on this lovely 'Water Hyacinth' are highlighted by gold and velvety-violet at the top of each blossom. Two-to-five-inch lime-colored leaves form clusters of rosettes. Photo by Carolyn Uber.

When we picture water plants, the colorful water lily usually comes to mind first. However, by planting various types of aquatics, your pond will take on its own unique look. Four main groupings of aquatic plants in and around the pond offer their own beauty and characteristics:

- *Plants that float on the surface and have roots submerged in the soil, such as water lilies and water hawthorne.*
- *Plants that remain totally submerged, such as oxgenating grasses.*
- *Plants that float on the surface and have roots dangling in the water, such as duckweed and water hyacinth.*
- *Plants that grow in wet soil at the water's edge of the pond such as cattails, and irises.*

Some of the criteria used for selecting plants in landscapes can also be applied to waterscapes. Keep in mind the clear water balancing formula that includes two bunches of oxygenating grasses and one medium to large water lily for each square yard of surface area. Other factors to

51

consider are growing conditions, growing space, plant height, foliar color and textures, and flower shapes and colors.

Water garden suppliers may be your best friend, not only in the early stages of designing your pond, but also in plant selection. They can tell you which plants will grow best in your region, where to plant them, and how to plant them. If your pond is properly constructed and stocked, you'll have years of enjoyment and little money lost through unfortunate plant choices.

Since most of today's gardeners are looking for low-maintenance gardening, the following lists of aquatic plants represent those that are the easiest and most successful for both home gardeners and commercial landscapers.

(Please note Chapter Five for complete information on water lilies.)

OXYGENATING GRASSES

Oxygenating grasses, one of the pond's most important aquatics, remain totally submerged. Sufficient oxygenating grasses will make it difficult for algae to flourish. Oxygenating grasses serve as food for your fish. In addition, the foliage serves as a bed to receive the spawn or eggs of fish and provides protection for the baby fish until they can fend for themselves.

Following is a list of oxygenating grasses most commonly used in garden ponds:

Myriophyllum

Miniature sagittaria

Anacharis

Sagittaria sinensis

*Vallisneria
(Used in lakes where overgrowth may be a problem).*

Cabomba

ORNAMENTAL GRASSES

Ornamental grasses are surface floating plants with their roots dangling in the water. Not only do they add a decorative touch to the pond, but they also provide a spawning ground and food for the fish.

Ornamental grasses offer the pond another service by being strong phosphate and ammonia removers. For this reason, they're frequently planted at the base of waterfalls. These grasses also help to keep the pond free of algae by competing for the nutrients and sunlight. They are easy to grow and require regular maintenance to keep them under control.

Each of the following ornamental grasses has specific characteristics which allow them to produce well in one region while not surviving as well in another. Check with an aquatic plant supplier if you have questions about specific plants for your area.

PARROT FEATHER *(Myriophyllum aquaticum)* - As an evergreen, native to South America, Parrot Feather leaves grow in thick whorls around their stems, rising six- to eight-inches above the water. Dainty cream-colored flowers appear in early spring, and in the late summer the tips of the leaves turn crimson. Parrot feather is a hardy and vigorous growing plant.

PRIMROSE CREEPER *(Ludwigia arcuta)* - This North American perennial has bright yellow flowers. Growing without stocks, the blossoms emerge from emerald-colored leaves.

DUCKWEED *(Lemna minor)* - Known as the second smallest aquatic flowering plant, this free-floating annual doesn't require planting. Plants set in the water will soon begin spreading. During the months of May and June, tiny blooms appear.

The bright lemon-colored blossoms of the 'Primrose Creeper', a prolific North American perennial, accent the pointed emerald-colored leaves.   Photo by Carolyn Uber.

The milk-white petals of 'Pennywort' rest on emerald-green leaves. This aquatic produces a three- to six-inch lacy curtain that shades and shelters fish.

Photo by Carolyn Uber.

SMALL FLOWERING AQUATICS

Small flowering aquatics are floaters with their roots in submerged soil. These plants not only add beauty to the pond, but they are also beneficial in other ways. They shelter your fish, help purify the water, and some are edible in salads or other dishes.

PENNYWORT *(Hydrocotyle umbellata)* - Resembling a miniature lotus, pennywort grows rapidly and stays green all year. As an excellent filtration plant, pennywort aids with nitrogen or phosphate problems. Planted on the sides of the pond, it also helps erosion. Five, tiny, white petals form a star-shaped bloom, resting on top of the emerald-green leaves.

FOUR LEAF PENNYWORT *(Hydrocotyle umbellata)* - Once planted along the bank or in the pond, this type of pennywort, shaped like a four-leaf clover, quickly produces a 3- to 6-inch thick mesh of plant material that shades and shelters the fish. In shallow water, this evergreen plant grows from 4- to 6-inches tall.

WATERCRESS *(Rorippa nasturtium-aquaticum)* - This hardy, filtrating, perennial thrives in sun or shade at the edge of the pond. It aids the pond with its oxygenating capabilities and acts as a nitrogen and phosphate remover. The small, rounded leaves and delicate, white flowers and stems can be used in salads or as a garnish.

WATER HAWTHORNE *(Aponogeton distachyus)* - A heavy bloomer, this native South Africa perennial, will cover an area three-feet in diameter and bloom in heavy shade. Its leaves float on the water, and in the warmer climates two- to four-inch waxy flowers appear in late summer when the water lilies begin going dormant. Depending on its age and the time of day, the blossoms display different hues and tones, from maroon-colored tips to crimson or garnet tones.

WATER HYACINTH (*Eichhornia crassipes*) - Some growers call this the plant of the future because of its amazing versatility. Water hyacinth bulbs contain methane gas, a possible source of energy in future years. Frequently used to purify ponds, this South American native also has a high food value and is used as cattle feed. Although the water hyacinth floats on the surface with its roots dangling in the water, it grows best when planted in containers or tub gardens where it can be controlled. A six-inch stock with lavender-colored flowers emerges from a cluster of two- to five-inch leaves.

WATER POPPY (*Hydrocleis nymphaeoides*) - Resembling its namesake, the California poppy, this South American perennial is easy to grow in sunlight and shallow water. Three-petaled, lemon-colored flowers perch above small, oval or heart-shaped green leaves.

BOG GARDEN PLANTS
'Japanese Arrowhead', 'Oxygenating Grasses', 'Cattail', and 'Water Irises' are perfect bog garden plants. For instructions on building a bog garden, see page 158.

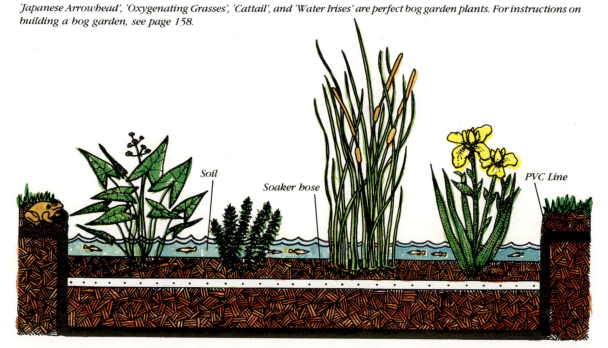

AQUATIC PLANTS

'*Montevidensis*', *a South American native, has arrow-shaped leaves and, in the summer, numerous small creamy flowers.*

Clockwise from Top Left: The umbrella structured foliage on the tall and stately 'Umbrella Palm' accents the beauty of other aquatic plants.; The 'Japanese Arrowhead', so named because its leaves are shaped like arrowheads, is a striking water garden addition.; Lovely purple flowers on the 'Azure Pickerel' aquatic plant add color to the pond from early summer through fall.; 'Papyrus' aquatics serve as a border along the shallow sides of the pond.

BOG PLANTS

Bog plants are inhabitants of the wet soil near the edge of your pond or in water up to 6-inches above the soil. Some ponds are stocked with bog plants only; however, these tall plants with their vertical lines offer an attractive contrast when planted nearby the flat, rounded pads of water lilies.

In addition to bringing another dimension of beauty to your pond, bog plants also serve some useful purposes.

Some of the blooms such as cattails are natural for fresh and dried flower arrangements. The Chinese water chestnut, another bog plant, produces nut-like fruit that can be used in many oriental and continental dishes.

The most practical and aesthetic method of using bogs in the pond is to plant both deciduous and evergreen types. Plant the two types close together, thereby making it less noticeable when the deciduous bog plants die off.

56

AZURE PICKEREL PLANT *(Pontederia lancifolia)* - This North American deciduous aquatic plant blooms freely from early summer through fall. It grows well in boggy soil at the water's edge or in the shallow portion of your pond. The glossy, long, olive-colored leaves may reach 4-feet in height with 3 -to 4-inch spikes of sapphire-colored flowers.

CATTAIL *(Typha latifolia)* - This high-decorative, deciduous resident of Europe, West Asia and North America can grow as tall as 8-feet. The cattail, a rapid spreader, likes still or slow-moving water or banks. The velvety, brown, cylindrical blooms are frequently used in indoor arrangements.

CHINESE WATER CHESTNUT *(Eleocharis dulcis)* - The deciduous Chinese water chestnut grows freely in shallow water and produces a nut-like fruit that is edible in a variety of dishes. The cylindrical, emerald green foliage extends upwards to 2-feet out of the water.

PAPYRUS (Cyperus papyrus) - This evergreen aquatic plant, used since Egyptian days as paper, is considered a tropical. These plants can grow up to 6-feet tall, and they are usually interspersed with other bog plants to break up the waterscape.

HORSETAIL RUSH *(Equisetum hyemale)* - Easy and quick to grow, the equi-setum, an evergreen, has creeping rootstocks that help watery banks hold firm. Tall, thin, hallow, jointed stems rise up to 4-feet high and sometimes bear cones.

GRACEFUL CATTAIL *(Typha angustifolia)* - This deciduous, smaller version of the cattail reaches 2- to 3-feet in height and fits well in most waterscapes. It provides a spawning ground for fish and produces a multitude of velvety blooms for use in floral arrangements.

HAIR GRASS *(Eleocharis acicularis)* - Native to Europe, Asia and North America, hair grass produces coffee-colored flowers in the summer and autumn. Its trailing roots sprout rush-type leaves, 2- to 12-inches long. Hair grass, an evergreen, grows in clumps and provides a spawning ground for fish.

JAPANESE ARROWHEAD *(Sagittari japonica)* - This deciduous aquatic plant, with leaves shaped like an arrowhead, is found in shallow ponds, rice fields, and along streams in most areas of the world. The Japanese arrowhead thrives in wet soil or in water no deeper than 6-inches. It rarely gets taller than 3-feet. During the

AQUATIC PLANTS

'Water Irises' come in an assortment of colors -- violet, cream, wine and yellow. Their broad, emerald-green leaves are shaped like swords. Water Irises produce year-round foliage as opposed to deciduous aquatics such as 'Cattail'.

summer months, the plant produces numerous tiny, three-petaled, white blossoms.

MINIATURE PAPYRUS *(Cyperus haspan vipiparus)* - This 2- to 3-foot evergreen plant grows profusely in sun or partial shades in warm climates. Rising from masses of winding roots, clumps of leaves display flowers with clusters of sepals. The flowers turn from pale chartreuse to tan.

MONTEVIDENSIS *(Giant Arrowhead - Sagittaria montevidensis)* - Very similar in appearance to its smaller relative, the *Japanese arrowhead*, this deciduous aquatic will attain a height of 1- to 4-feet when planted in wet soil or water no deeper than 6-inches. This South American native has arrow-shaped leaves, and in the summer produces numerous small creamy flowers.

UMBRELLA PALM *(Cyperus alternifolius)* - A Madagascar native, the umbrella palm likes marsh ground or shallow water and full sun. This evergreen aquatic is a beautiful pond plant if kept under control. The slender, leaf-sheathed stems with masses of 4-to 8-inch long leaves rise 2- to 4-feet above the water. During the summer months, small carmel-colored blooms appear in the midst of the leaves.

WATER SWAN (*Alisma gramineum*) - This unusual looking perennial plant, which looks best in dirt lakes, has leaves that assume a swan-like appearance as they reach maturity. The water swan bears tiny, delicate ivory blossoms on long stems.

WATER IRIS

Water iris plants grow well around the edges or in the shallow areas of your pond. All water irises have broad, emerald-colored leaves shaped like swords. These plants should be fertilized heavily in January for spring blooms.

BLUE IRIS (or BLUE FLAG) - Violet blossoms, some with streaks of yellow, green and white; bloom in early summer.

DR. BIRDSEY - Large, creamy flowers with lemon-colored centers.

ROSE RED IRIS - Rose wine-colored blossoms; blooms spring and summer.

YELLOW IRIS (*Pseudacorus*) - Canary-yellow flowers; grows well year-round.

LOTUS

The lotus, a large deciduous water plant that grows wild in many parts of the United States, requires plenty of growing room in large ponds or lakes and frequent fertilization to grow at its best. Although the lotus can withstand a cold climate if the rootstocks don't freeze, a humid climate is its best growing condition.

The lotus buds emerge around the end of July and stand above the pond almost 2-feet on strong stems. Large, cup-shaped, pale yellow petals encase the seed receptacle. After a few days the petals fall and the pod and its seeds begin maturing and enlarging, turning brown in color.

Designs of the beautiful 'Lotus' flower have been uncovered in archeological diggings and in ancient tombs and temples.

AQUATIC PLANTS

(These attractive seedpods are valued in dried flower arrangements.) Around the end of September these seeds fall back into the pond and can lie buried, sometimes for several years, until the seed opens and a new plant begins to emerge.

Once established, the lotus plant grows downward during the winter, forming tubers below the frost line. Although these tubers are temperamental for shipping purposes, many people the world around successfully maintain lotus plants in their water gardens.

LOTUS SEED PROPAGATION - The lotus may be propagated by following these instructions:

- *In early May, drill the seeds just enough to break the outside protective coating at opposite points.*
- *Cover the seeds with water and set the container in the sun.*
- *Change the water weekly.*
- *If the seeds are properly drilled, they should sprout in about one week.*
- *Place the sprouting seeds in a pot of soil in a sunny, open area of the pond below the water 6-inches to*

18-inches. In about 2- to 3-weeks the 2" wide lotus pads emerge.

CARE OF YOUR PLANTS

When To Plant

WARM CLIMATES - While most of us start taking a good look at our yards and gardens during the warmer spring months, fall is actually the best time to plant a pond. Nature has begun slowing everything down and algae is less active than in the spring. With a fall constructed pond, you'll have a ready-made garden, alive with color and activity, when the weather warms up in the spring.

COLD CLIMATES - Early spring is the best time to plant a pond in cold climate regions.

How To Plant

For most ponds, planting in containers is preferable to placing soil in the bottom of the pond. However, if you prefer to plant directly into the soil on the pond bottom, anchoring the plants in the soil is important. Sheets of wire mesh embedded in the soil will usually provide the necessary stability.

Container planting allows you to vary the depths as required for the different plants, and makes pruning, fertilizing and cleaning the pond easier.

Plants grow extremely well in paper (pulp) planters. These containers hold up under water, allowing nutrients and fresh water to pass into the plants' root systems. Cover the holes with 2-ply newspaper to keep the dirt in the container.

Submerged soil is not intended to provide air or store water, but rather it provides the plant with nutrients. Use only topsoil in the containers, making sure it does not contain insecticides or herbicides. Do not use potting mixes, peat moss, compost or steer manure. Prepare your planters by filling 1/2 full with a mixture of good garden topsoil and a granular fertilizer,

following the directions on the package. Fill to the top with soil. You may want to cover the soil with a fine layer of sand to prevent it from spilling out into the water. Excessive sand can injure the plant's roots.

Once planted, following the instructions for each type of plant, slowly lower the container to the suggested depth. If the plants are too deep, prop the container up with bricks or blocks.

Oxygenating Grasses

Oxygenating grasses cannot be allowed to dry out. Either plant in prepared and positioned containers under water in the pond itself or plant the aquatics while they are submerged in a large container of water,

By using containers, aquatic plants are able to grow at their varied growth rates. They also make fertilizing and repotting easier.

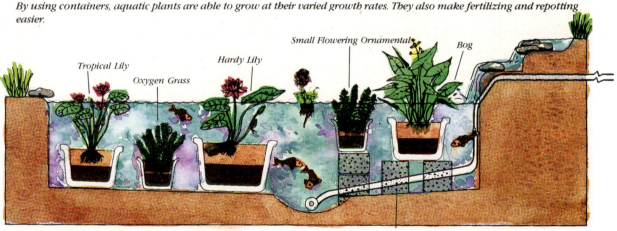

Small Flowering Ornamental

Bog

Tropical Lily

Hardy Lily

Oxygen Grass

Blocks for height control

Fertilizer   Soil   Cement Blocks

AQUATIC PLANTS

then transfer to the pond.

Since grasses are foliage feeders, many do not have roots. Place the trimmed end in the soil, making sure the bunches of grasses are centered in a 6-inch diameter/6-inch deep container and firmly planted one-third into the soil. Use two bunches per planter and place the container on the bottom of the pond, distributing the planters throughout. Use two bunches of grasses for every 100-gallons of water.

If the pond has green water when adding the grasses, raise the pots so these plants will receive sunlight under water. As the pond clears, lower the pots to the bottom of the pond.

In ponds where fish eat the grasses, isolate the grasses in a screened off area until the plants mature, then spread them throughout the pond.

Ornamental Grasses

Ornamental grasses cannot be allowed to dry out. Either plant in prepared and positioned containers under water in the pond itself or plant the grasses while they are submerged in a large container of water, then transfer to the pond.

For 6-inch diameter/6-inch deep pots use two bunches per container. Plant the ends of the grasses firmly in the center of the planter. Place containers in the pond so that the soil line is 3-to 6-inches below the water.

Small Flowering Aquatics/Bogs

Depending on your plant selections, two container sizes are generally used for planting small flowering aquatics and bogs: 6-inch diameter/6-inch deep containers or 15-inch diameter/8-inch deep containers. Use one plant per 6-inch container and 3 plants per 15-inch container. Place the containers in the pond with 4- to 8-inches of water over the soil line.

Lotus

Lotus tubers need rich soil and plenty of room. Cover the lotus tuber with 2-inches of soil at the heavy end and extend the growing end above the soil 1/2-inch. (Take care not to break or damage the growing end or the plant will die.) Lower the container into the pond until it's covered by 2-inches of water. As the lotus grows, gradually increase the water depth to 6- to 12-inches.

PRUNING YOUR AQUATIC PLANTS

Periodic removal of old or excess foliage is important to the health of your plants. A good rule to follow on pruning is not to prune more often than once a month. Your aquatic plants should have ample time to draw nutrients back from the foliage into the tubers or rhizomes.

**Oxygenating Grasses/
Ornamental Grasses**

When thinning out the oxygenating grasses, never remove more than 10-percent at any one time, wait a month and remove another 10-percent, and so on. Wait until June or July before you begin removing oxygenating grasses. As spring gets underway and the pond comes to life, these grasses are essential for pond balance.

Small Flowering Aquatics/Bogs

Small flowering aquatics can overgrow and become a problem when the pond is too rich in nutrients, while in fresh, clear, balanced ponds these plants will remain under control.

These aquatic plants can be kept under control by removing the excess plants on a monthly basis. With a sharp knife, cut and remove an entire root section, usually no more than 10-percent per month. The second month remove another 10-percent, continuing this foliage removal until the plant is manageable size. Trimming only the edges may lead to matting and rotting of the old foliage.

Papyrus plants are known to have grown along the Nile in Ancient Egypt. These 'Miniature Papyrus' offer an interesting contrast when planted nearby the rounded pads of colorful water lilies. *Photo by Carolyn Uber.*

FERTILIZING YOUR AQUATIC PLANTS

Most aquatic plants receive sufficient nutrients from the fish and the pond. Without fish, fertilization is required. Voracious fertilizer consumers, such as water lilies, will require regular fertilizing. If the leaves begin turning yellow, the plant may need fertilizing.

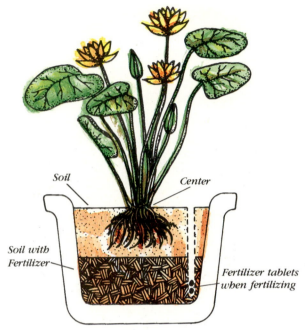

Soil

Center

Soil with Fertilizer

Fertilizer tablets when fertilizing

Feeding the Tropical Water Lily - Using an old broom, make a hole in the soil and insert an aquatic fertilizer as shown.

45° angle

Fertilizer tablets when refertilizing

Feeding the Hardy Water Lily - Using an old broom, make a hole in the soil and insert an aquatic fertilizer as shown.

Use only aquatic-type fertilizers sold by water gardening suppliers. These carefully balanced fertilizers should be used during initial pond planting and all re-potting when new soil is added. Aquatic plant fertilizers encourage growth and more blossoms in deeper colors. Soluble fertilizers are seldom used since they cause a sudden burst of algae growth.

 Water Lilies

WATER LILIES

Upper Left, clockwise: 'Albert Greenberg', 'King of the Blues', 'Janice C. Wood', 'Mr. Martin F. Randig'. Photo by Gene Sasse.

When most of us picture a water garden, we think of water lilies and rightly so. The beautiful water lily, or *Nymphaea*, is recognized the world over. In fact, water lilies are indigenous to most countries in the world.

Not only are the beautiful water lilies considered the stars of the pond, but they perform several important functions. Their large round pads, which spread over the surface of the pond, reduce water evaporation, help the pond from breathing too fast, keep the water cool, and provide shade for fish. These attractive aquatics also produce oxygen in the water by photosnythesis.

Botanically related to the buttercup and magnolia, the original water lilies were white or sometimes a pale shade of pink. Today, through hybridization, water lilies bloom vibrant shades of purples, yellows, blues, coppers, and reds

Water lilies are divided into two basic groups: hardy and tropical. Tropical water lilies are further divided into day-blooming and night-blooming types.

In contrast to the hardy water lily, tropical varieties exhibit larger, taller blossoms with a wider range of colors and

Two tropical, day-blooming lilies developed by Martin E. Randig -- 'Eldorado', one of the largest yellow tropical water lilies and 'Enchantment' with delicate salmon-pink blossoms set off by speckled forest-green leaves.   Photo by Clint Bryant.

Right: The amethyst blossoms and variegated leaves of 'August Koch' complement the pale blue color of 'Blue Capensis'. Photo by Gene Sasse.

Left:Teaming up to make an eye-catching combination are 'Pink Star' and 'Yellow Dazzler', two beautiful favorites.   Photo by William C. Uber.

larger more colorful foliage. They are also easier to hybridize and considerably more fragrant than the hardy water lilies. Although color selection of the hardy water lily may be somewhat limited, many water gardeners appreciate them because they are not as sensitive to adverse weather conditions. For most gardeners a combination of both types of water lilies creates a well-rounded water garden – the tropical for color and the hardy for year round stability.

You'll find noticeable variations in the prices of water lilies. Generally speaking, the inexpensive water lilies propagate easily, while the more exotic and rare water lilies are somewhat difficult to propagate and therefore more expensive.

A water gardening supplier or consultant can help you select the proper water lilies for your pond and climatic conditions. If it's impossible to visit a water garden supplier, use the telephone. If you relate your needs, the supplier can offer immediate advice.

Since color selection is usually the number one consideration when selecting water lilies, you'll find each group – day-blooming, tropical night-blooming, and

hardy – alphabetized within color groupings. Keep in mind that the colors are only approximations. Variations in growing conditions will slightly affect the color of each plant's leaves and blooms.

A complete listing of all water lilies would be impossible since there are hundreds of varieties and new introductions every year. However, the following lists represent those plants most commonly found at water gardening suppliers.

TROPICAL DAY-BLOOMING WATER LILIES

Tropicals are considered annuals, although some of the day-blooming types will survive mild winter climates. The blooming season lasts from June until the first frost or until December in frost-free areas.

Not only is the tropical water lily floriferous, but the blossoms are large and vividly colorful. The flowers are held on stems rising out of the water from 6- inches up to 18-inches. The flowers of the day-blooming tropicals open full around noon and close up at dusk. The large leaves, which spread out over the pond surface, are occasionally viviparous (capable of

Day-blooming amethyst-colored 'Tina' grows well with 'Attraction', a garnet-colored hardy and 'Hermine', a cotton-white hardy. Photo by Clint Bryant.

'Red Star', a tropical, day-blooming lily, rises 12-inches above its large, deep-green leaves.   Photo by William C. Uber.

A favorite with water gardeners the world around, 'Pink Star' rises 18-inches above the water amid its large light-green leaves.   Photo by William C. Uber.

sprouting minatures of themselves).

Blues and purples are the strongest of the tropicals. Since white and yellow colors are usually the weakest plants in the tropicals, beginners may prefer to select these colors from the hardy water lily selections.

Star Lilies

Star water lilies have been around for years. They are different from the newer hybrids in several ways. The new hybrids have condensed foliage with shortened stems and larger flowers, while the old-fashioned stars have long stems, small leaves and small flowers, although they bloom well. Since star water lilies have a tendency to overrun, they are best suited to large ponds or lakes.

BLUE STAR - Long-time favorite of water garden enthusiasts. Its delicate violet-blue blossoms are accented by blue stamens and a golden center. This medium bloomer can grow in semi-shaded areas.

PINK STAR - Also called Stella Gurney, this ideal background plant rises 18-inches above water. The blossoms on this fragrant medium blooming plant are soft pink with a hint of lavender.

PURPLE STAR - This fragrant, medium blooming, violet-blue water lily stands high

Left: Also known as "Blue Beauty", 'Pennsylvania' is prized by water gardeners for its huge, blue blossoms highlighted by black dotted and lined sepals and bright yellow stamens. Photo by Dennis Tannen.
Right: 'Margaret Randig', a Martin E. Randig creation, blooms large, lightly blue flowers with blue-tipped sepals. Photo by William C. Uber.

'King of the Blues' appropriately describes this majestic, navy-colored day-blooming tropical water lily. Photo by Clint Bryant.

above its large leaves.

RED STAR - Also called Mrs. Ward, this medium blooming water lily is deep pink with brilliant crimson stamens. Its narrow, tapering petals form an almost perfect star, 8 to 10-inches in diameter.

ROSE STAR - As one of the most fragrant star lily varieties, it provides medium blooms during a long growing season. Deep rose-purple blossoms stand tall above the large leaves.

WHITE STAR - This medium blooming, highly fragrant water lily is an attention-getting addition to any pond. Huge, pure-white flowers contrast with large, slightly mottled leaves.

Blues

AUGUST KOCH - This versatile tropical water lily produces delicate amethyst blossoms in small or large ponds and in sun or semi-shade. The huge green leaves, tinted pink underneath, are viviparous. The highly fragrant blooms are frequently used for indoor arrangements.

BLUE CAPENSIS - This hybrid is a prolific bloomer all year around. The delicate pale blue petals cup around a yellow center.

71

WATER LILIES

BLUE PYGMAEA OR COLORATA - A light bloomer, this highly fragrant water lily is almost navy-blue in color. It is adaptable to both tub gardens or large ponds as well as semi-shaded surroundings.

BLUE SMOKE - This sky-blue lily with its silvery fluorescent sheen and large red-brushed leaves is dramatic in any pond. It blooms well throughout the season.

CHRISTINE LINGG - Beginners do well with this hybrid water lily. The blue flowers shaded with lavender bloom lavishly during the growing months.

CLINT BRYANT - This hardy, deep purple-blue petals and gold centered water lily will grow in semi-shaded areas. It is recognized as one of the tallest stemmed of all tropicals.

DAUBEN - This water lily has won awards for its versatility and beauty. Its small, fragrant blooms have lemon-yellow centers, white sepals, and narrow blue petals with green underneath. A hardy tropical, it is ideal for small pools, tub gardens, or indoors. The heart-shaped, green leaves are viviparous.

MARGARET RANDIG - Huge, faintly-blue, broad petals cluster around blue-tipped yellow sepals in this highly fragrant

The deep jade-green leaves of the 'Edward D. Uber', introduced by Van Ness Water Gardens in 1985, makes a perfect background for the beautiful, electric-purple flowers.
Photo by Dennis Tannen.

flower. This water lily can be planted in semi-shaded areas and blooms in winter if placed in a greenhouse. The leaves are dark green and heavily variegated.

PAMELA - This hybrid is an excellent bloomer with saucer-shaped, broad, sky-blue flowers.

PENNSYLVANIA - Also known as Blue Beauty, this is an excellent all-round water lily. The *Pennsylvania* is prized for its huge, deep-blue blossoms highlighted by black dotted and lined sepals and bright yellow stamens with violet anthers. The fragrant flowers stand 8-inches above slightly brown-speckled leaves and sometimes grow as large as 2 feet in diameter. It grows well in

'William C. Uber', named for the author of this book, produces a multitude of beautiful crimson flowers.   Photo by Clint Bryant.

WATER LILIES

small pools and can grow in semi-shaded areas.

SACRED BLUE LOTUS OF THE NILE - For the experienced water gardener, this blue tropical will grow in semi-shaded areas.

ZANZIBAR BLUE - As one of the standard water lilies, it adapts readily to any size container and can grow in semi-shaded areas. Deep-blue blooms are accented with numerous crimson stamens.

Dark Blues

DIRECTOR MOORE - This versatile hybrid, which grows in any size pool including tub gardens, is a good water lily for beginners. It has several blooms at one time with amethyst petals and bright gold centers. The dark green leaves are flecked with purplish brown on top and pure purple underneath.

KING OF THE BLUES - Prized for its beauty, it is one of the most popular hybrid water lilies with navy petals clustered around gold, blue-tipped sepals. An excellent bloomer, it is easy to grow and can be planted in semi-shade.

LEOPARDESS - An outstanding sapphire color, it is complemented by heavily variegated leaves. It blooms during winter in a greenhouse and adapts to any

size planting container.

MIDNIGHT - This unusual hybrid is easy to distinguish from other tropicals with its slightly crinkled, deep-violet blooms. It may be planted in semi-shaded areas.

TINA - The long, slender amethyst petals of this hybrid fade to a lighter shade near the gold center which is highlighted by deep amethyst-tipped sepals. As one of the best water lilies on the market, it reproduces and blooms well; adapts to any size container; will grow in semi-shade; and propagates by bulb, seed, or leaves (viviparous).

This fragrant, magenta-colored 'Evelyn Randig' blossom stands out against the unusual large leaves which are a mixture of chestnut and purple spots and stripes on a background of green.   *Photo by Clint Bryant.*

Purples

EDWARD D. UBER - The electric-purple flowers with pink shades surrounding a golden center are set off by deep, jade-green leaves. It grows well in all locations including cool and shady ponds (up to 60-percent shade). The leaves are viviparous.

MRS. MARTIN E. RANDIG - Plum-colored petals, crimson sepals and a banana-yellow center combine in a study of contrasts. This versatile water lily, with its viviparous leaves, adapts to semi-shaded conditions and any size planting container.

Roses

EVELYN RANDIG - The leaves, a mixture of chestnut and purple spots and stripes, are as beautiful as the magenta-colored blooms. It blooms constantly during the season.

MR. MARTIN E. RANDIG - Long, ruby petals are set off by lightly blotched forest-green leaves. This heavy blooming water lily stands out in a crowd.

ROSE PEARL - This hybrid exhibits huge, garnet-colored blooms. The plant provides abundant blooms during the growing season.

'Pink Capensis', a lovely bloomer throughout the season, produces fragrant, shell-pink blossoms.   Photo by Dennis Tannen.

The pink petals of 'Persian Lilac' are almost violet in color with a mass of pink-tipped stamens in the center.   Photo by Clint Bryant.

75

WATER LILIES

The gently rounded petals of day-blooming tropical 'Ted Uber' are clustered around a soft yellow center.   *Photo by Clint Bryant.*

The gorgeous tropical day-blooming 'Louella G. Uber' displays pure white, fragrant blossoms.   *Photo by Clint Bryant.*

TAMMIE SUE UBER - The fuchsia-colored petals contrast with a delicate gold center and forest-green foliage. This highly fragrant flower is an excellent bloomer.

WILLIAM C. UBER - The multitude of highly fragrant, crimson flowers are complemented by large, deep-green leaves. As a hybrid this water lily is a good bloomer.

Pinks

ENCHANTMENT - The unusual, delicate salmon-pink color makes it stand out in any pond. A heavy bloomer, it likes a crowded pond and opens early in the day.

GENERAL PERSHING - This is one of the finest water lilies ever produced. It blooms huge, richly scented, orchid-pink flowers all day long. The flowers stand 14-inches above purple lined, green leaves splotched red underneath. The plant adapts well to small ponds.

LEADING LADY - A medium blooming yet strong growing plant, this large, multi-petaled, peach-pink water lily adapts to any size planting container. The flowers open fully and lie flat on this medium blooming plant, even under artificial light.

PERSIAN LILAC - This fragrant, multi-petaled, almost a semi-double bloom flower has violet-pink petals with pink-tipped golden stamens. It is a good water lily for beginners.

PINK CAPENSIS - This hybrid, a good bloomer throughout the season, has shell-pink blossoms with yellow centers. The large green leaves are slightly mottled.

PINK PEARL - A good bloomer throughout the season, this tropical has silver-pink petals tipped with deeper pink and yellow stamens. It may be planted in semi-shaded areas.

PINK PERFECTION - An excellent bloomer, this water lily is a good one for beginners. The delicate pink blooms with their pink-tipped yellow stamens are highly fragrant. The large, brown and green leaves are heavily variegated.

Whites

JANICE C. WOOD - This hybrid has beautiful marshmellow-white petals tipped with amethyst and a bright gold center. The blooms contrast with the vivid green and maroon variegated foliage. It blooms heavily during the season.

MARIAN STRAWN - Vanilla-colored petals extend from a buttercup center and form an almost perfect star. This is a good all-round water lily with huge blossoms that bloom profusely from morning until night during the season.

LOUELLA G. UBER - This pure white, highly fragrant water lily blooms continuously during the season and remains open when other day blooming lilies have closed up for the night.

Amber, peach, pink and topaz blend in perfect harmony in the flowers of 'Afterglow'.   *Photo by Clint Bryant.*

Set above emerald green leaves, 'Yellow Dazzler' blossoms large, bright yellow flowers.   *Photo by Clint Bryant.*

WATER LILIES

MRS. GEORGE PRING - The large, 13-inch, star-shaped, creamy white flowers with bright yellow and white-tipped stamens stay open from early morning until dusk. Although the leaves, green and mottled with reddish brown, are large, this hybrid water lily is suitable for small ponds.

TED UBER - This water lily with its large, semi-double, cloud-white flowers is adaptable to large or small ponds. It is also good for lakes because of its striking color and size.

Tropical, day-blooming 'JoAnn' blossoms vibrant raspberry red flowers that look like sparkling jewels in the pond. Photo by Clint Bryant.

Yellows

ELDORADO - This hybrid is one of the largest yellows. The heavily variegated leaves contrast with the lemon colored blossoms.

JAMIE LU SKARE - This good, all-round water lily is an excellent bloomer. The butter-colored blossoms are highly fragrant.

ST. LOUIS GOLD - This colorful gold and yellow flowered hybrid is adaptable to large or small ponds, or tub gardens.

YELLOW DAZZLER - This tropical is one of the best. It blooms profusely throughout the season. The large, flat, bright yellow flowers are set above emerald-green leaves. It is adaptable to any size container.

MRS. CHARLES WINCH - With its unusual, asymmetrical shape, this tropical is hardy and a strong grower in any garden. The deep-lemon, star-shaped blossoms have four large outside petals and a cluster of smaller inside petals. The olive-colored leaves have tiny variegations.

Talismans

These unusual water lilies bloom yellow with red tips, then turn red as they mature. In a crowd of water lilies, they always stand out.

AFTERGLOW - This heavily fragrant, multi-colored water lily blooms profusely. It is versatile, adapts to any size container, and grows well in tub gardens.

ALBERT GREENBERG - This excellent blooming hybrid grows well in any size container and in large ponds or tub gardens. The cup-shaped blossoms have petals of gold and orange hues, and the leaves are mottled, avocado-green.

Reds

AMERICAN BEAUTY - The scarlet-colored flowers with gold centers bloom continuously throughout the season. The huge, rounded, kelly-green leaves reveal a brilliant red coloration, veined in green on the underside. This plant adapts well to most ponds.

JOANN - The vibrant raspberry-red petals which curl outward from a rich gold center are surrounded by deep crimson stamens. This highly fragrant water lily blooms profusely. It will also grow in semi-shaded areas.

JACK WOOD - This excellent blooming water lily is good for beginners. The flowers are raspberry-colored with a butter-gold center with ruby stamens and the avocado-colored leaves are lightly blotched. It will

A mass of raspberry petals gather around a butter gold center in the stunning 'Jack Wood' tropical.   Photo by Clint Bryant.

'Green Smoke' is known to gardeners as a truly unusual water lily with its chartreuse and pale-blue tipped petals.   Photo by Clint Bryant.

WATER LILIES

grow in semi-shaded areas.

Greens

GREEN SMOKE - This excellent blooming water lily is outstanding in looks, but difficult to grow. Extending from a bright yellow center are chartreuse petals which gradually fade into a pale blue at the tips. The extraordinary flower is set off by bronze speckled, wavy-edged, deep-green leaves. It adapts to any size container.

TROPICAL NIGHT-BLOOMING WATER LILIES

When the tropical day-bloomers fold up at dusk, the night-blooming tropicals take over. While the color selection in this group is smaller, the colors themselves range from brilliant reds to pinks and whites. Night-bloomers are especially effective in commercial settings such as hotels and

When day is done and the sun fades beyond the horizon, beautiful night-blooming 'Wood's White Knight' becomes the star of the pond.
Photo by Carolyn Uber.

restaurants where patrons are apt to be passing by. One or two lights focused on these flowers will give any garden pond a night-time profusion of color. However, these flowers do need full sun during the daylight hours.

Reds

H.C. HAARSTICK - These large, 12-inch, brilliant carmine-colored blooms will flower during winter if protected from the cold. Red-gold stamens and coppery-red leaves complement this night-blooming hybrid.

RED FLARE - This night bloomer is the top-of-the-line in reds. The fragrant, vermilion blooms are set amid mahogany foliage. It will flower during winter if placed in a greenhouse.

MRS. JOHN A. WOOD - An eye-catching water lily with its maroon blooms and leaves. It is adaptable to any size planting container.

Whites

MISSOURI - This old water lily with its large chalk-white, multi-petaled flowers that grow up to 14-inches has been popular for years. This water lily is a winter bloomer if placed in a greenhouse. It adapts to any size container.

Night-blooming 'H.C. Haarstick' casts its brilliant carmine flowers upon the evening waterscape. Photo by Carolyn Uber.

SIR GALAHAD - One of the best of the white water lilies, this plant, with flowers of sugar-white petals and bright goldenrod centers, blooms prolifically and stays open from dusk until almost noon of next day.

WOOD'S WHITE KNIGHT - A prolific bloomer, this night bloomer produces vanilla petals accented by lemon-tipped stamens. Its emerald leaves are variegated underneath and have scalloped edges.

Roses

MRS. GEORGE HITCHCOCK - Soft-rose petals are accented by mahogany stamens which reach to 12-inches in size in this hybrid. It is adaptable to any size container and blooms in the winter if placed in a greenhouse.

The sugar-white 'Sir Galahad' blooms prolifically and stays open from dusk until almost noon of the next day. Photo by Clint Bryant.

Pinks

MRS. EMILY HUTCHINGS - This profuse pale coral-pink night-bloomer with its unusual bronzed leaves adjusts well to tubs or other containers. It will bloom during the winter if placed in a greenhouse.

HARDY WATER LILIES

Hardy water lilies are everything their name suggests. They'll live for years even in the coldest climates. In fact, as perennials, hardy water lilies require a period of winter dormancy and seldom need winter protection unless the pond freezes.

Left: Soft, gently curving, pale coral-pink petals set off 'Mrs. Emily Hutchings' against unusual bronzed leaves. Photo by William C. Uber.
Right: Perfected by hybridizer John Wood, 'Mrs. John A. Wood' draws immediate attention with its maroon-colored blossoms and leaves. Photo by William C. Uber.

Hardy water lilies bloom from June to October in cooler climates and April to October in the warmer climates. The flowers stand just above the water level and are available in various shades of pink, red, white and orange from miniatures to huge flowers.

Hardy water lilies differ from the tropicals in root structure. Their tuberous root system is called a rhizome, a creeping stem that lies horizontal under the surface of the soil. The rhizome is solid and black in color. As the rhizome ages, it toughens to withstand weather changes and survive cold winter months.

In order to survive mail-order shipment, hardy water lilies arrive as bareroot plants without foliage. It takes four to six weeks after planting for these water lilies to become established and bloom. The first few blossoms are not always true in color. Give the hardy water lily some time for its true color to emerge. Color intensity is affected by soil conditions, fertilizer quantities, amount of sunlight, and climate conditions.

Yellows and whites are the strongest colors in hardy water lilies. The dark red hardy water lilies will burn in desert climates.

The hardy water lilies noted herein are considered the easiest to grow for both home gardeners and commercial landscapers.

Mild Pinks

MARLIAC CARNEA - This is one of hardiest water lilies with excellent color and blooming capabilities. The vanilla-scented blossoms are soft shell-pink and the large, wine-colored leaves gradually turn to forest-green as the plant grows. It is well-suited to any size pond, particularly lakes, and grows in partial shade.

MORNING GLORY - This good, hardy water lily opens its large, pink-coral blossoms early in the day.

Miniature Pinks

SUMPTUOSA - This highly fragrant, strawberry-pink hardy is a good all-round miniature. The stamens are a golden red color.

Pinks

FORMOSA - The delicate, pale-pink flower with lemon stamens is a long-time favorite. It is an excellent bloomer and adaptable to planting containers.

LUSTROUS - This is one of most attractive hardy water lilies with its huge, rose-pink blossoms, canary-yellow stamens and chocolate and pink sepals. It is an excellent bloomer all season long.

MASANIELLO - White sepals and amber stamens accent the carmine-dotted, rose petals which deepen with age. The foliage is a forest-green. The plant will grow in semi-shade.

PINK SENSATION - This heavily fragrant rich-pink water lily has oval-shaped, long petals and parrot-green leaves tinted red beneath. It stays open later than most hardy water lilies.

ROSY MORN - The shell-pink petals form a star on this heavily fragrant hardy. It is an excellent bloomer.

SPLENDIDA - A Marliac hybrid, this excellent bloomer has ruby blossoms and spinach-shaded foliage. It is a good hardy for beginning water gardeners.

Left: The blossom on 'Pink Perfection' stands out among the variegated leaves in the backyard pond of the McDaniel's home. Photo by Gene Sasse. Right: Although formal in construction, this pond within a brick patio gives a comfortable, informal look. Photo by Clint Bryant.

Bottom Left: The hardy 'Marliac Carnea' water lily blooms profusely in ponds of all sizes. Photo by William C. Uber.

Bottom Right, Clockwise from Top Left: Color is usually the number one consideration when selecting water lilies. Photo by Fran Clemence.; The 'Pink Capensis' blossom stands majestically tall among the leaves. Photo by Carolyn Uber.; The large green leaves of these tropical water lilies spread over the surface of the pond. Photo by Clint Bryant.; Water lilies perch regally, sometimes as much as 18-inches, above the water on their graceful stems. Photo by William C. Uber.

Opposite, Top: Backyard gardens can become havens of relaxation with the addition of a pond, fish and aquatic plants. Opposite, Bottom Left: The blossom of the 'Marliac Carnea' stands out against the deep green leaves. Opposite, Bottom Right: 'Pink Perfection' stands out in any pond with its heavily variegated leaves and delicate pink blossoms.

WATER LILIES

Yellows

MARLIACEA CHROMATELLA - This universally favorite hybrid has canary petals with mustard stamens and pink-tinted sepals set on a pale sulfur background. Delicately scented, the blossoms are set against bronze-marked, olive leaves. It is adaptable to semi-shaded areas and with its medium size blooms is a nice addition in tub gardens.

ORDORATA SULFUREA - This hardy is an excellent bloomer with numerous slender sulfur-colored petals, which darken with age, light goldenrod-hued stamens and chocolate-blotched leaves. It can be planted in semi-shade and grows well in tub gardens.

PYGMAE HELVOLA - The bright yellow miniature blooms seldom grow over 2-inches in diameter. The small, olive-green leaves are distinctively marked with cocoa and maroon streaks and blotches. It is a perfect hardy for small ponds and tub gardens.

SUNRISE - The huge, sun-colored blooms stand tall out of the water over large forest-green, red-flecked leaves. An excellent bloomer, it adjusts well to semi-shaded areas.

Sunsets

COMANCHE - This hybrid is unusually colored. Apricot-colored when it first opens, the next day it's a coppery-red with canary-yellow outer petals and persimmon stamens. The leaves change from plum to chocolate-speckled green. It is a prolific bloomer and adjusts to semi-shade and any size container.

PAUL HARIOT - This heavily fragrant flower is used for indoor arrangements. It opens as a canary-colored blossom and gradually turns scarlet as it matures. The flowers stand tall over crimson-spotted emerald-green leaves. It can be planted in semi-shaded areas.

Reds

ATTRACTION - This award-winning hybrid has large, garnet petals flecked with white and tipped with rose; its white sepals are traced with rose and its stamens are a mixture of mahogany and amber. An excellent hardy for beginners, it grows vigorously and blooms profusely almost anywhere. It is also adaptable to semi-shade.

CONQUEROR - This older hardy is still strong and popular with its large, watermelon-colored petals flecked with vanilla and banana-colored stamens. Although not suitable for desert climates, it grows well in all sizes of ponds.

ESCARBOUCLE - When its fragrant blossoms first open, the petals are a brilliant vermilion with gold-tipped, garnet stamens. As the days pass, the blooms deepen to a wine and crimson.

FROEBELI - Its highly fragrant, fuchsia flowers with vermilion stamens and canary anthers sit among marbled, red-edged, parrot-green leaves.

Right: The soft shell pink blossom of the hardy 'Marliac Carnea' stands out against the forest green leaves.
Below: The 'Marliac Carnea' blooms profusely and grows equally well in small ponds, tub gardens and large pools, whether they're in full or partial sun.

WATER LILIES

As recipient of the Royal Horticulture Society's "Award of Merit," 'Marliac Albida' displays spectacular white flowers with softly rounded petals.

At daybreak the hardy 'Morning Glory' opens its breath-taking large, coral pink blossoms.

Whites

FLOR DE BLANCA - This is an excellent, hardy water lily for large ponds and lakes. The blooms are cotton-white with canary centers and pointed petals.

GLADSTONIANA - This award-winning lightly fragrant hardy has waxy, cup-shaped petals of coconut-white and golden stamens. The large, circular leaves are forest-green. It can be planted in semi-shaded areas.

GONNERE - The white, broad petals of this double flowered hardy have canary stamens and olive-colored sepals. It adjusts to any size planting container.

HAL MILLER - One of the largest white-blossomed hardies, it needs to be kept under contol. An excellent bloomer, it grows well in semi-shade.

HERMINE - The small to medium-sized blooms on this hardy have emerald-green sepals and foliage. It grows in any size container and can grow in semi-shade.

MARLIAC ALBIDA - This award-winning, spectacular white-flowered plant is one of the few fragrant hardy water lilies. The sepals have a touch of pink and are centered by bright yellow stamens. The leaves are emerald-green on top and light pink underneath. It is a healthy grower and bloomer.

VIRGINALIS - This water lily is considered the best hardy on the market by many. Its large blooms, up to 12-inches in diameter, are pure white from the first day of the blooming season until the frost arrives. The pure white of the shell-shaped petals is broken by canary-colored stamens and rose-hued sepals. An excellent bloomer, the flowers with their long blooming season last in indoor arrangements.

Left: Truly a rainbow water lily, 'Comanche' appears apricot colored when it first opens and the next day, it turns a coppery red with canary yellow outer petals.
Right: A universal favorite, 'Marliacea Chromatella' is not only a beautiful yellow blossomed lily, but it is extremely hardy and will weather the coldest of winters.

A kaleidoscope of changing colors can be found in this award-winning hardy hybrid, 'Attraction'. Large garnet petals are flecked with white and tipped with rose.

The huge, fragrant, sun-colored blossoms with long, narrow curved petals on the hardy 'Sunrise' rise slightly above large forest green leaves with red-flecked cocoa beneath.

This hardy water lily has been properly cut and cleaned prior to planting at a 45° angle.

— — — — — *Trim foliage*

VICTORIA REGIA

No discussion on water gardening would be complete without mentioning the amazing *Victoria regia*, correctly called *Victoria amazonica*, the gigantic water lily first discovered in South America. Its huge leaves stretch 5- to 6-feet across with turned up edges that add an additional 5- to 7-inches. The unusual formation of the underside of the leaf creates exceptional buoyancy. In fact, one leaf can hold up to 200 pounds. Its fragrant, multi-petaled

blossoms measure from 15- to 18-inches in diameter. Unfortunately, these large night-blooming blossoms only last a couple of days.

The *Victoria amazonica* is easy to grow, although it meets with greatest success in the warmer, humid climates. Rather than forming a tuber or rhizome like other water lilies, the *Victoria amazonica* is generally grown from seed, which has been started in 85-degree to 90-degree water.

Transportation of these plants presents problems since their briars are toxic and they can die if their leaves touch each other. (They are not toxic to humans.)

'Gladstoniana' is a study in perfection with its white, waxy, cup-shaped petals clustering around gold-colored stamens.

This beautiful assortment of hardy water lilies includes (top left, clockwise) 'Sunrise', 'Virginalis', 'Comanche', and 'Masaniello'.

CARE OF YOUR WATER LILIES

When to Plant

Where you live and the climatic conditions affect the timing for planting water lilies. Tropical water lilies may be planted after the last frost in your area. Check this date by calling your state's Department of Agriculture or your local water garden supplier. The ideal temperature for

The excessive roots and pups have been pruned on this tropical water lily for re-planting.

planting tropicals is when the water reaches 70-degrees F. or above and 60-degrees F. for hardy types. Hardy water lilies may be planted either while in active growth, or during their dormancy period.

Tropical water lilies are shipped as bare root plants but suffer little setback, so they often bloom within a few days after planting. If an unexpected cold snap does occur, protect your tropicals by covering the pond or by bringing the new plants inside.

Tropical water lily bulbs can be stored for the winter, following the instructions in Chapter Nine.

How to Plant

Ideal cultivation for all types of water lilies includes planting in full, direct sun, with good topsoil and slow-release fertilizer. The more sun, the more blooms.

For most ponds, planting water lilies in containers is preferred to placing soil in the bottom of the pond. Container planting allows for easier fertilizing, pruning, and pond cleaning. Plug all holes in the containers with 2-ply newspaper. Plants grow extremely well in paper (pulp) planters. These containers hold up under water, allowing nutrients and fresh water to pass to the plants' root systems.

Water in the garden. It brings us refreshing coolness on the hottest summer day. It satisfies our senses with sound that only water can make. It delights our eyes with the unsurpassed beauty of water lilies, the glimmering iridescence of fish and reflections from the sky above.   *Photo by Carolyn Uber.*

All bare-root water lilies should be dipped into a rooting concentrate before planting to aid in the plant's establishment.

Water lilies cannot be allowed to dry out during the planting process. Either plant under water in the pond itself after you've prepared and positioned the container, or plant the water lilies while they are submerged in a large container of water, then transfer to the pond.

For maximum growth and flowers, water lilies should be planted in the largest container possible. They need a minimum of 3-cubic feet of soil. Ideally the planter

WATER LILIES

should have 6- to 8-inches of water over the soil line. If the pool is deep, prop the container up with blocks or bricks. If the pool is shallow, use a shallow planter and do not have less than 4-inches of water over the soil line. In ponds with limited sunlight, water lilies should never have more than 6-inches of water over the soil line.

Hardy water lily rhizomes are planted at a 45-degree angle against the side of the planter with the crown (the portion of the rhizome where the stems of the leaves and buds originate) 1/4-inch below the soil and facing the opposite side of the pot.

Tropical water lily bulbs are planted in the center of the planter with the crown out of the soil. You'll note a white line on the tropical plant. This soil line tells you the depth for planting. If the line is not noticeable, plant the roots in soil to the crown.

Check the plants in 5 days to make certain that the dirt has not packed away from the crown and roots.

Re-Planting Bulbs/Rhizomes
HARDY WATER LILIES - Cut and remove pups 5-inches back from the crown.

Prune any tubers extending over the sides of the container and all small suckers on the water lily plant.

Before replanting, cut the rhizome tuber down to 5-inches, remove the hair roots and trim off the foliage.

Although the foliage should be removed, this illustration shows the proper method for planting the hardy water lily.

Remove all foliage that is uncurled. Remove roots with a sharp knife. Wash and clean the root. When re-planting make certain the root crown is 1/4-inch below the dirt surface. Check the root again in 5 days to make sure that the dirt has not packed away from the crown.

TROPICAL WATER LILIES - If you followed the instructions in Chapter Nine on storing tropicals for winter, you can re-pot them next spring. Watch your pond plants for new growth. When you notice new growth in the pond, remove the bulbs from the sand packing. Rinse the bulb carefully, taking care with the new sprouts. Fill a clean container 1/2 full of water. Place the bulb in the bottle of water in a warm, sunny spot. Replenish the water as needed, until the bulb sprouts.

Once sprouted, plant the bulb 1/4-inch below the soil line with the smooth side down. Polarity is important. Make certain that the sprouts are facing up, and place the pot 4-inches below the pond surface in a sunny area until the leaves get 5-inches in diameter, then drop to 8-inches below the pond surface.

In warmer areas where the tropicals continue to grow throughout the winter, re-

Water has a relaxing affect, whether it be the rhythmic waves of the ocean, a gently running brook, or the quiet beauty of a pond. We may be unable to recreate oceans and brooks, but we can find pleasure in building and stocking a water garden. Photo by Hildegarde Mitchell.

potting is much simpler. Mid-spring, remove the pot from your pond. You will notice that the tropical plant has extended itself straight up and out of the pot on a tuberous type of root. Measure the distance from the dirt level to the top of the tuber, or where the leaves extend. Take the rooted mass out of the pot and cut off that distance from the bottom of the root mass.

WATER LILIES

Place the plant back into the pot and refill with dirt and fertilizer, covering the crown with 1/4-inch of dirt. Place the pot back in the pond in a warm, sunny spot with 4-inches of water over the pot. The new roots will appear from the crown. If your fish eat these new roots, cover the pot with 1/2-inch wire mesh.

Pruning Your Water Lilies

Pull your water lily pots up once a month. If the lily's foliage is bunching in the center, remove a 12-inch diameter section to let light to the crown. Leave three or four crowns in the pot.

Once a month remove the dead foliage, taking care not to rid your pond of all the snails. Snails lay their eggs, a clear jelly-like substance, on the underside of water lily leaves.

Fertilizing Water Lilies

Since water lilies thrive on fertilizer, they should be fed with a tablet fertilizer monthly during the spring, summer and fall for maximum performance, or quarterly at the minimum. Use only aquatic-type fertilizers sold by water garden suppliers. These carefully balanced fertilizers should be used during initial pond planting and all re-

potting when new soil is added. Aquatic plant fertilizers encourage growth and more blossoms in deeper colors.

Propagating Water Lilies

VIVIPAROUS PROPAGATION

Water gardeners who wish to propagate water lilies will find the project easily accomplished with viviparous plants.

"Growing like a leaf" takes on a special meaning to water gardeners who have learned that many tropical water lily leaves reproduce their entire plants. Water lilies may be propagated from these viviparous leaves. Photo by Gene Sasse.

Viviparous is a term for mature leaves that sprout miniatures of themselves in the center space where the petiole joins the lamina. Tucked out-of-sight beneath the leaf are tiny root and tuber systems for new plants.

VIVIPAROUS FOLIAGE
Miniature water lily leaves begin to sprout from within the mature leaf.

You may propagate lilies from these viviparous leaves by carefully detaching the miniatures from the mature leaves with a sharp knife. Often several miniatures are involved so it is best to separate each before planting. Firmly plant each little miniature in rich soil, either in a shallow pan/dish or a 3- to 4-inch clay pot. Then place the container in shallow water.

Plants produced from viviparous leaves develop into full-size varieties, and they are able to withstand moderately cold weather better than most tropical lilies propagated from seeds or tubers.

SEED PROPAGATION FOR TROPICALS
Propagation of some types of tropical water lilies is possible by seed. Following completion of the bloom, collect the

'Panama Pacific', a viviparous tropical water lily, buds a deep, bronze color flecked with rust, then opens full as a wine-colored blossom highlighted by purple tipped yellow stamens. Photo by Clint Bryant.

WATER LILIES

enlarged seedpods and place them in a container of water until the pod breaks open. Since water lily seeds are tiny, they should be filtered through a small-mesh screen in order to separate them from the pieces of seedpod. You can either store the dried seeds for later use, up to two seasons, or sow in soil in small pots and place in shallow water. After the seedlings appear, they can be transplanted to the pond.

Plant Problems

Water lilies, particularly the hybrids, have few problems. They are highly resistant to disease and pests. Aphids and cutworms occasionally present problems, but can be controlled by using a 5-percent solution of Ortho's Volck Supreme Oil Spray on all foliage in and near the pond. The best deterrent for pests is an overhead water spray, such as electric irrigation system, that nightly wash the plants' foliage.

This illustrated 'tuberosa odorata', without a central crown and root system, shows the structural difference between the older water lilies and the newer, hybrid water lilies, as shown in other illustrations.

Foliage extends back on root

CHAPTER 6

Fish

FISH

Koi in a water garden.   *Photo by Carolyn Uber.*

Although fish are not absolutely necessary to pond life, those people who introduce fish into their water gardens have indeed added new dimensions as well as color and movement. But more importantly, these pond owners have added new friends. Fish friends are easy to care for. They won't tear up your yard, and you don't have to worry about feeding them when you go away.

In addition to offering new dimensions to your pond, fish also serve an ecological purpose by acting as pond gardeners, trimming excess plant foliage and eating algae, mosquito larvae, aphids, flies and other insects. Since a balanced pond with sufficient, established plants provides their basic diet, you'll only use fish food as a reward and in small amounts.

These Pinecone, Ohgon and Platinum Koi serve as pond gardeners, helping to keep the pond free from algae. Photo by Carolyn Uber.

These Tri-Color and Ohgon Koi add color and movement to the water pond.   *Photo by Carolyn Uber.*

Fish are important for balancing the newly-constructed pond. However, in the beginning the fish should be small in size and few in quantity. As the plants begin to stabilize, more fish may be added. These new fish will become established within the pecking order and soon your pond will interact as a total unit.

FISH

EXTERNAL PARTS OF FISH

In order to better understand fish and their needs, let's take a closer look at our cold-blooded vertebrate friends.

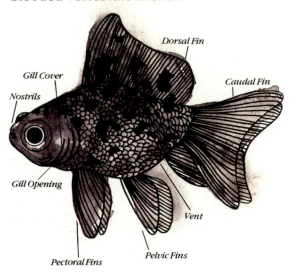

Dorsal Fin

Gill Cover

Nostrils

Caudal Fin

Gill Opening

Vent

Pectoral Fins

Pelvic Fins

TYPES OF POND FISH

Some fish are more suited for pond life than others. Aquarium or tropical fish are not adaptable to pond life. Following are some types of pond fish you may wish to consider:

KOI *(Japanese Imperial Colored Carp)* - Koi or Goi are the most popular pond fish, and for several good reasons. They are intelligent, hardy, responsive to humans and come in a beautiful array of colors.

The Golden Ohgon makes a colorful addition as do the Pinecone and German Scale Koi in water gardens of all sizes.   *Photos by Carolyn Uber.*

Koi should be kept in shallow 1-1/2 feet to 4 feet ponds with concrete, fiberglas, PVC or dirt bottoms. Although Koi can tolerate temperatures from freezing to 90 degrees, they will not endure rapid temperature variations.

More Koi are sold than any other single fish. Prices vary considerably depending on the grade. Good healthy pond Koi may be purchased for a few dollars, while show-quality Koi can run several hundred dollars.

Hundreds of years ago the Japanese categorized the Koi. These categories continue to exist, although over the years new colors have developed and some Koi hobbyists have expanded these guidelines.

102

Koi are generally grouped as follows: (1) Hikali Mono (brightly colored); (2) Doitsu (German; large-scaled or scaleless); Taisho (basic color either white or red); (4)Showa (basically black); and (5) Asagi (basically blue).

In recent years, Koi have been developed into metallic golds, silvers and coppers, brilliant tri-color combinations, blues, lemon yellows, bright oranges, and platinum whites.

The life cycle of Koi in a pond is about 10 to 15 years. The oldest recorded Koi is over 200 years.

GOLDFISH *Carassius Auratus* - As another member of the carp family, goldfish have been popular pond livestock over the years. While these fish are not as responsive and trainable as Koi, they are easy to care for. Koi and goldfish can be mixed in your pond.

If your climate has wide variations in temperature, you may want to consider goldfish, since they withstand these variations better than Koi. If your pond is small, goldfish should again be your choice. They don't require as much exercise or oxygen as Koi.

Make certain when selecting goldfish

The Fantail Goldfish, an exotic member of the carp family, is not recommended for the outdoor garden pond. Photo by Dennis Tannen.

that you are buying stock bred for pond use. Comets or Shubunkins, a type of goldfish, are the popular choices for ponds. These colorful tri-color or red fish with large fins and tail development are quite active and require the added space provided by a pond. Exotics such as Moors and Fantails often do not do well in ponds.

The life cycle for pond goldfish is about 10 to 15 years.

GUPPIES/MINNOWS/MOSQUITO FISH - These small fish multiply quickly and are only recommended for tub gardens, shallow ponds,or ponds that are bothered by animals. They are adaptable to temperature and surface area fluctuations.

FISH

Water gardeners should remember that large Koi have large appetites.　　　*Photo by Carolyn Uber.*

GAME FISH - While game fish are not suited to garden ponds, they can be an asset to natural lakes or large man-made ponds as might be found on commercial golf courses. Game fish should not be considered in ponds under 100,000 gallons of water and will do best in lakes of over 500,000 gallons. These fish grow large and need plenty of exercise. They also need the cool temperatures offered by large bodies of water.

Game fish such as Catfish, Blue Gill, and Bass are handled and regulated by the United States Fish and Game Department. Contact this department if you are interested in stocking game fish.

Two other fish, Golden Orfe and Talapia, may be restricted in some areas. Check with your local Fish and Game officials before importing these fish.

SELECTING YOUR FISH

The most important factor to remember when selecting your fish is to pick out the ones you like. It's your pond and your fish. Since fish are pets, look for the colors, scale patterns, and characteristics that appeal to you. Be as selective with fish as you would be in looking for other pets – puppies, kittens and birds.

Select fish that are healthy, active and alert. Make sure they are not deformed or physically damaged in any way.

When choosing either Koi or goldfish, select ones who have just reached maturity in the 4" - 5" size. The mortality rate under that size is about 80 percent. The difference in age between a 4" - 5" fish and a 10" - 12" is six to twelve months.

Large Koi, who have probably been fed fish food three times a day, have large appetites. Once they are placed in the pond, they may eat all your plants. A basic rule to remember about feeding your fish is that each time you add or subtract something from the pond, you take a chance of disturbing its ecological balance. Also keep in mind that the more you feed your fish, the more they eat and the larger they grow, again disturbing the pond's balance.

The quantity of fish you select for your pond should follow specific rules. The surface area of the pond breathes in carbon dioxide and releases oxygen, making the surface area more important than the total gallons of water contained in the pond. The basic rule for quantity in a newly-established pond is no more than 8" - 10" of fish per square yard of surface area. In other words, two 4" - 5" Koi or goldfish for each square yard of surface area will allow room for growth and breeding without overcrowding. Mature ponds (over 120 days or balanced) can handle 15" of fish per square yard.

FROM THE HATCHERY TO THE POND

Koi that arrive on the marketplace have been carefully screened. From their beginnings at the hatchery to their introduction to your pond, they have been inspected for physical deformities, coloring,

105

FISH

scales and size. A continuous culling process goes on at the hatchery, not only for quality, but also to genetically upgrade fish.

During the culling process about 75 percent of the fish are used as feeder fish, leaving the balance to be separated into one of three grades. Grade #1 fish are the top-of-the-line. These show-quality fish are judged by their color conformity, exactness of patterns and color intensity. Many from this group will be saved for the next breeding season. Grade #2 fish are healthy fish. Their patterns may be less than perfect, but color intensity is usually good. Grade #3 fish are less than perfect in color intensity.

After making your fish selection at an aquatic supply center, the fish will be netted into plastic bags containing a small amount of water, then filled with oxygen. Do not put the plastic bags in the trunk or sunshine, or it will be too hot for the fish.

When you arrive home, immediately place the bags, still closed, into the pond and allow them to float in the water. This allows the water temperature inside the bags to gradually reach the pond temperature. If the bags are floating in the sun, cover with wet towels to protect the fish from too much heat. After the bags have floated for 20 to 40 minutes, open and let the fish swim out. By allowing a gradual temperature change, your fish will not be suddenly shocked, which may weaken their resistance to disease.

Having barely survived the traumatic experience of being tossed around at the hatchery, packed in shipping boxes, netted several times then packed up again for the trip to the pond, these frightened fish will stay hidden for several days or weeks. For the first two or three weeks while your fish are hiding, use food tablets as a bribe. Throw one food tablet on the surface of the pond at the same time each day. Fish

Intermittent rewarding keeps your Koi friendly and responsive *Photo by Carolyn Uber.*

become excited at any surface agitation. It tells them that a food source, such as a bug or fly, has hit the surface. Even if they don't respond at first, keep the rewarding procedure up at the same time each day. Usually, they'll be out of hiding within 10 days.

If, after these 10 days pass, you still receive no response, a heavier rewarding program may be necessary. For 5 days at the same time each day, throw in one food tablet every minute for five minutes. If after 5 days that still doesn't work, pull up a chair, relax and throw in one tablet every minute for 20 to 30 minutes. You seldom

Koi and Goldfish can be mixed in the garden pond, although Goldfish are not as friendly as Koi. Photo by Carolyn Uber.

will have to reach this point. If you do, there may be a cat, dog, or bird in the area scaring the fish.

Cut back on the rewards, once your fish respond. Intermittent rewarding keeps your fish responsive from this point on.

BREEDING IN THE GARDEN POND

Breeding time for both Koi and goldfish is spring and early summer with hot days and cool nights. The female fish, her body swollen with eggs, swims about rapidly depositing her eggs. The male chases after her, fertilizing the eggs. Fertilized eggs are amber in color and unfertilized are white. If these eggs aren't hidden, they will be eaten.

With sufficient plant life for spawning, most pond fish will breed regularly. Ideal pond plants for breeding include oxygenating grasses, parrot's feather, water hyacinth and other small ornamentals.

If your pond doesn't have sufficient plant life, you can provide a spawning ground by placing a new mop head in the pond during February or March. This allows ample time for the mop head to build up algae before the spring breeding. Once

107

FISH

Koi and Goldfish feed on algae on the side of the pond.
Photo by Carolyn Uber.

eggs have been laid within the mop head, remove it to a separate tank where you can raise the small fry.

The small fish fry will hatch in 5 to 7 days, but remain hidden until they are 3" - 4" and have developed their colors. At this size, culling is an important process to save your basic fish. Just as the hatcheries cull, pond gardeners must do likewise. Discard fish that are weak, deformed or unattractive to you. Always keep in mind the size of your pond in relationship to the number of fish

(8" - 10" of fish for each square yard of surface area).

When you notice the breeding process going on, give the pond a salt treatment. (Thoroughly mix 1/4-pound of formulated fish salt or sea salt containing anti-bacterial agents with one-gallon of water for each 100-gallons of pond water. Evenly distribute over the pond.) The males become aggressive during breeding and may injure themselves or the females on the rough edges of the pond. A salt treatment, which won't hurt the eggs, is a good healer and a wise preventative measure for curbing diseases that may occur during this stressful time.

TRAINING YOUR FISH

Goldfish occasionally become friendly with their owners, but they don't develop the same close attachment that Koi have for people. Koi have distinctive personalities and can be trained to eat from your hand and do simple tricks as well as intricate tricks.

Food becomes your training device, just as it was used to bring your fish out of hiding. By throwing one or two food tablets in the water at the same time each day, the fish begin responding to YOU. Food is used only as a reward, not as a steady diet. Once they've learned to surface on command, you can develop a rapport and begin training your fish. They will soon surface to you rather than for the food.

Koi are highly responsive. They want to be your friend and respond to you. Begin playing with them - put your fingers in the water, pet them, play with them, move your finger in a circle and they'll soon be making a circle, too.

The training process may take some time, depending on how well you and your fish respond to each other. Once you have made friends with your Koi, you have made a friend for life. Even though they may be abused, overheated or stressed, they will survive because they are your friend. Koi have been known to die if they think they have been abandoned by their human friend.

DISEASES AND TREATMENTS

Although pond fish rarely become sick and diseased, the following information will help owners if a problem develops:

- *If your fish are dying one at a time over a long period of time, they are usually diseased. Immediate death of several fish probably means toxic levels of chemicals.*
- *None of the diseases or parasites that affect fish are contagious to humans.*
- *Ailments are similar among all fishes and most ailments are treatable if prompt action is taken.*

The sooner you treat the disease or problem, the sooner you can reduce the mortality rate. Since speed is important in curing your fish, a small first aid kit of salt and vitamins is important. The suggested Salt/Vitamin treatment will get you through most emergencies (animals getting in the pond, accidental draining, etc.) Salt is a universal healing agent and will not harm the fish or plants.

SALT-VITAMIN TREATMENTS

SALT TREATMENT (Formulated fish salts or salts with anti-bacterial agents) - For each 100-gallons of pond water, throughly mix 1/4 pound of salt into one gallon of water. Distribute evenly over the pond.

VITAMIN TREATMENT - For each 100-gallons of pond water, mix 2 drops

FISH

liquid vitamins into one gallon of water or as per label instructions. Distribute evenly over the pond.

45-DAY POND TREATMENT

The following 45-Day Pond Treatment will usually cure most fish ailments and diseases. (If problems persist, check with your local aquatic supplier.)

DAY 1:

A.   Mix thoroughly in a gallon of water 1/4 pound of formulated fish salts per 100-gallons of pond water. Distribute evenly through pond.

B.   For each 100-gallons of pond water, mix 2 drops of vitamin-based solution into one gallon of water or as per label instructions. Distribute evenly throughout pond.

DAY 2: For each 100-gallons of pond water, thoroughly mix a sterilant-based product into a gallon of water as per label instructions. Add to the pond after 6:00 p.m.

DAY 5: Repeat Salt Treatment

DAY 8: Repeat Sterilizing-based Treatment

DAY 10: Repeat Salt Treatment

DAY 15: Repeat both Salt and Sterilizing-based Treatments

DAY 20: Repeat Salt Treatment

DAY 22: Repeat Sterilizing-based Treatment

DAY 25: Repeat Salt Treatment

DAY 29: Repeat Sterilizing-based Treatment

DAY 30: Repeat Salt Treatment

DAY 35: Repeat Salt Treatment

DAY 36: Repeat Sterilizing-based Treatment

DAY 40: Repeat Salt Treatment

DAY 43: Repeat Sterilizing-based Treatment

DAY 45: Repeat Salt Treatment

Early recognition of a sick or diseased fish is sometimes difficult. Frequently, an illness won't be detected until the first fish dies. By then all the fish have been affected in one way or another. Watch for any of the following signs of illness:

- *Gapping*
- *Sunken Eyes*
- *White spots on the body*
- *Listing or sluggish*
- *Dorsal fin down*
- *Stomach sucked in or bloated*
- *Veins bursting in fins and gills*
- *Bubbles on the skin*

When water districts began improving their water qualities, many of the previously common fish diseases and illnesses were eliminated. Check a fish disease book or your aquatic supply store if you have problems with tail rot, anchor worm, lice, or leeches. Today, fungus and Ich may still occasionally occur.

FUNGUS - Parasitic fungus is present in almost all ponds, but healthy fish are usually resistant. This disease appears on the fish as patches of white film, appearing on physically damaged areas, then attacking the surrounding tissue.

Because fungus is so highly contagious, isolating one fish does little good. The entire pond and all the fish should be given a Vitamin Treatment immediately, followed with the 45-Day Pond Treatment.

ICH *(Ichthyophthirius)* - This white parasite penetrates the surface skin of the fish and feeds on the tissue. Immediately treat the pond and fish with a Vitamin Treatment, followed by the 45-Day Pond Treatment.

HANDLING THE INJURED OR SICK FISH - Fish are delicate creatures, so unless you're past the novice stage, you may do more harm handling one fish than by treating the entire pond with fish included.

ESTABLISHING A HEALTHY POND

Pond conditions and stress factors that may affect the welfare of your fish include: ammonia toxicity, gas problems, chemical poisoning, introducing new fish into an established pond, and changing the pond water.

AMMONIA TOXICITY - This condition causes much of today's illness in fish. If you overfeed your fish, the food starts building up on the bottom of the pond. It becomes a biological sewer of food, fish waste, dirt, microcosm and bacteria. These elements begin breaking down in the form of gas ammonia, which is toxic to your fish.

Temperature is a factor with ammonia toxicity. In colder temperatures, ammonia is not usually a problem, but when temperatures go up over 72 degrees, everything speeds up, including the breaking down of the pond's natural elements.

An ammonia test kit may be purchased to check the pond water. When concentration of higher than one part per million ammonia exists, the pond should be treated with ammonia removers purchased from

FISH

your local aquatic supplier.

For ammonia toxicity, immediately give the pond a vitamin treatment followed by a salt treatment every 5 days for 15 days.

GAS PROBLEMS - Improper balances of oxygen or carbon dioxide will affect the fish. During the natural photosynthesis process the highest concentration of oxygen occurs from 11:00 a.m. to 6:00 p.m., and the highest carbon dioxide from about 1:00 a.m. to 9:00 a.m.

Gas problems usually occur in the spring when the pond may be overstocked or the fish are feeding heavily after the long winter months. When the veins in the fins or gills begin bursting or when the fish begin gapping, particularly in the early morning hours (6:00 a.m. - 7:00 a.m.), this usually indicates a gas problem.

If a gas problem is evident, immediately add oxygen to the pond. Place a pump in the pond with the outlet about 1" below the water surface. The pump should create white water, indicating a high oxygen content. Run the pump continuously, but particularly from 1:00 a.m. to 9:00 a.m., when oxygen is at its lowest point. Usually the pump is only necessary for two to three weeks, while the pond goes through this transition. Also give the pond an immediate Vitamin Treatment, followed by a Salt Treatment every 5 days for 15 days.

CHEMICAL POISONING - If death comes quickly or you begin to lose your largest/fastest fish, the problem may be chemical poisoning from metals, herbicides, insecticides, or toxic plants. If the toxic level is low, the fish may be weak and listless.

To prevent metal poisoning, use metal-based algaecides following label instructions. Since these products work on an oxidation process, air temperature will affect the chemical reaction. The warmer the weather, the faster the algaecide works. All chemical spraying, whether by you or your neighbor, should be done in the early morning before there is a wind drift.

Treatment for chemical poisoning will depend on severity. If an herbicide or insecticide has accidentally sprayed onto the surface of the pond, overflowing may correct the problem. Overflow no more than 2 percent per hour for 48 hours, followed by a Salt/Vitamin treatment. If it's a heavy dose of chemicals, the pond should be drained and rinsed, following the suggestions below for "Changing the Pond Water."

INTRODUCING NEW FISH TO ESTABLISHED PONDS - As fish make their home in your pond, they build up a natural immunity to many of the elements in their habitat. However, when you add new fish to this habitat, these newcomers may readily pick up diseases from the pond. For the welfare of all the fish, old and new, a Salt Treatment and Vitamin Treatment will be necessary.

CHANGING THE POND WATER - If it becomes necessary to move your fish to clean or treat the pond, be certain that the water temperature is the same in the secondary pond. Use the same pond water unless it's been contaminated. If fresh water

After a few years, Koi may revert to their natural colors.   *Photo by Carolyn Uber.*

FISH

is used, treat it with a chlorine remover and a Vitamin/Salt Treatment.

A child's wading pool, placed in the shade, can serve as a temporary home. Depending on the temperature and water quality, the fish should not remain in the temporary pond any longer than 60 to 120 minutes. If the fish begin gapping, they must be returned to their pond, or immediately aerate the temporary pond with a pump.

If your pond cleaning and/or repairing will take longer than two hours, your bathtub may be used as a fish tank. Treat the water with vitamins and salt. Refresh 25 percent of the water twice a day. Fish may be fed while they are housed in the bathtub.

At other times when you are changing more than 25 percent of the pond water, or working on the pond or plants, a Salt/Vitamin Treatment will again be necessary as a preventative measure against fish injury.

DISPOSING OF FISH

A final warning about disposing of fish should be issued. Keep fish in their proper habitat. If you decide you don't want your fish, take them to a pet shop or animal shelter. Do not introduce your pond fish into lakes, streams, or other natural bodies of water. Ecological problems develop when fish are introduced into areas which are not their natural habitat. Most local laws prohibit people from placing exotic fish into natural bodies of water.

CHAPTER 7

Pond Residents And Visitors

Dragonfly.

Photo by Carolyn Uber.

When we create a water garden, whether commercially or in the backyard, we are building something that is alive and breathing. We are bringing nature into our environment and attracting animal life we may not ordinarily have an opportunity to enjoy.

From tiny microscopic creatures to dragonflies or snails, the pond is a never-ending and ever-changing cycle of life. Birds, bugs, frogs, and animals come to visit and drink from the pond. In many cases your pond is a neutral area for animals to gather for drinking and eating. You may find some of the creatures desireable, others you may not.

One joy in maintaining a pond is the awareness we acquire about the intricate relationship among pond animals. Each pond member, from dragonfly to fish, plays its role in making your pond its own unique habitat. In fact, your pond is at its prime when the greatest varieties of species co-exist.

SNAILS

Water snails are the small time gardeners in your pond. They slowly work their way over the foliage of bogs, water lilies, and grasses, removing the algae so the plants are kept clean for breathing and survival. (Algae particularly collects around the oxygenating grasses since both forms of plant life are competing for the gasses and nutrients in the pond environment.)

Many prospective water gardeners make erroneous assumptions about water snails. First, in most climates water snails do not eat your pond's decorative plants. The mainstay of their diet is algae, not plant material. Second, snails don't clean the bottom of the pond. They are no more interested in the pond sewage than anyone else. If you find snails on the bottom of the pond, they are probably dead. Third, water snails do not leave the pond. They live, eat, and reproduce within the confines of the pond structure. Fourth, snails will not overrun the pond. In a balanced pond, snails will balance themselves out. However, snails in overly warm environments, such as greenhouses with heaters, may eat the plants. Certain types of fertilizers also seem to stimulate the snails to eat plants.

As you observe the water snail, you will be amazed at his agility. Not only can he crawl almost anywhere he wants, but he can also turn on his pod, take in air, and float upside down on the water's surface until he finds a plant that catches his eye. He then releases the air and drops down on the foliage.

Snails have two main predators – man and fish. If you find that you are continually replacing the snails in your pond, you may be the cause. Snails lay their eggs, a clear jelly-like substance, on the underside of the water lily leaves. If you are constantly trimming these leaves, you are probably throwing away snail eggs. For some unknown reason, snails select the older leaves for laying their eggs, the ones we are likely to prune. The best suggestion is to inspect the leaves before pruning.

Fish can be another predator of snails. Small fish usually leave the snails alone. But, unfortunately many overfed fish, who reach 8" - 10" in size, will start going after the snails. Once one fish starts eating snails, the others will follow suit. In this case, rather than using snails to control the algae, you may have to give the pond an algaecide treatment. (See Chapter Three on "Setting Up a Pond.")

If you received your snails by mail

As the pond's small time gardeners, snails form a vital link in pond balancing. They neither leave the pond nor eat the leaves of the aquatic plants. Snails simply remove algae from the plants, keeping them clean for breathing and survival.

order, they will likely appear in hibernation when they arrive. Upon arrival, float the plastic bag and snails in the pond water for 20 minutes to equalize the temperature before releasing them into the pond. Treat the pond with a vitamin-based product, and if you are using new water, treat for chlorine and chloramines. Do not assume the snails have died until they have been in the pond for at least three days. Many times snails placed into a new pond will lay eggs then die.

TOADS/FROGS

Probably the friendliest and most

interesting creatures to take up residency in your pond will be the frog or the toad. (The toad may be more desireable since he makes little noise.) In many cases you may have trouble telling these two apart since both have bulging eyes and sit hunched up with back legs longer than the front. On closer inspection, you will find the frog's skin is smoother, without the warts found on toads.

The frog jumps while the toad hops, and adult frogs will stay close to the water, while the toad may be found outside the pond.

These two cold-blooded amphibians survive by adapting to variations in

Water gardeners look for the friendly frog, usually one of the pond's first visitors. You'll know he's there when you hear his nightly croaking song. As an amphibian, the frog can live both in and out of the water. Frog families can be started by acquiring some tadpoles.   *Photo by William C. Uber.*

temperature. During the hot weather they will stay near the coolness of the pond, and if the water freezes, they will bury deep into the mud and hibernate.

The eggs of these amphibians are laid in water, and the young spend the first part of their lives in the water as tadpoles or polliwogs. Although thousands of eggs may be laid and the pond appear to be overrun with tadpoles, few will survive. The life of the egg and the tadpole is not an easy one. The pond harbors a number of predators – water beetles, dragonfly nymphs, fish, birds, turtles, cats, and dogs.

Although tadpoles are voracious algae eaters, they won't eat your decorative plants. The length of time for a tadpole to turn into a frog depends on the weather and the species, from a few days to three years. During this metamorphosis the tadpole also changes from a vegetarian (algae) to a carnivore (insects and bugs).

When you acquired a toad or frog as a tadpole, he will probably stay in your pond for life. If introduced to the pond as a full-grown frog, he will usually leave. Also, your pond will only be occupied by the number of frogs or toads it can support.

DRAGONFLIES

One large insect, the dragonfly, is sure to catch the eye of all pond owners. Those who have watched the ugly, brown bug emerge from their pond and turn into a colorful dragonfly will admit that few of nature's phenomena are matched.

The dragonfly eggs are laid on the water surface and drop into the mud at the bottom of the pond. Once hatched, these tiny hatchlings, which resemble overgrown earwigs, go through several stages of larval development. The homely, greenish-brown nymph or naiad lives on the pond bottom, feeding on other aquatic insects. After one to three years, and 10 to 15 molts, the nymph is ready to leave the pond. The number of molts and length of time will vary according to the species. In a metamorphosis process the nymph crawls out of the water onto the stem of a plant. After a few hours the skin begins splitting across the head and down the back. From this opening the adult dragonfly emerges.

The adult dragonfly is a far cry in appearance from the nymph. Large eyes, with over 29,000 facets, can see in almost any direction. Heavily-veined wings extend out from the body when it rests, and the eye-catching, brilliant colors vary from a copper red to a peacock blue, depending on the species. The prey of the adult consists largely of flies, gnats and mosquitos.

SMALL INSECTS

It takes a practiced eye to spot the many small insects that find their homes in your pond. These small insects, for the most part, play a beneficial role in pond life by providing food for other pond animals. Bugs and insects are seldom a problem in a balanced pond, and mosquitos won't be a problem if you have fish.

Some insects such as midges, black flies, and mosquitos spend their early lives in the water and fly away when they become adults. Other fascinating little water insects keep the pond alive with movement. Whirligigs are dark, shiny little insects that spin in circles on the surface of the pond. The back swimmer, with a back shaped like the bottom of a canoe, propels itself by two, long oarlike hind legs. Water beetles, one of the pond's larger insects, feeds on decaying vegetation and other water insects, and water sow bugs may be seen crawling on the bottom of the pond. Crayfish, frequently

One popular visitor to the pond is the dragonfly, who's sure to catch your eye with his brilliant red and blue colors. Photos by Carolyn Uber.

Although beautiful to watch as they float around the pond, ducks should not be an addition to the water garden filled with plants and fish. Ducks should have a pond all to themselves.   Photo by William C. Uber.

found in dirt bottom ponds, will bore through the mud to make nests, which may cause drainage problems. The crayfish are also predators of fish and will cause stress among the pond fish. Other pond bugs include the water scorpion, red worms, and flatworms.

As mentioned earlier, each pond is individual in its makeup. The insects that find their way to your pond may be temporary visitors stopping by for a drink, or they may like the environment and decide to stay.

DUCKS/GEESE

The general consensus among long-time pond owners is that ducks and geese are

122

more trouble than they are worth in the pond. They are, in fact, considered manure manufacturers to many. These attractive nuisances munch away at everything from snails to plants.

DUCK POND - If you're truly interested in bringing ducks into your aquatic habitat, you will be wise to construct a separate pond, away from the fish and water lilies, for these feathered friends. Duck ponds require cement construction since they can tear up PVC-lined and PVC ponds capped with cement.

Place a drain in the bottom of the pond, running it to an outside overflow. With a constant source of overflow water and by piping from the bottom, you can keep the waste material cleaned up. Water hyacinths, planted around the edge of the overflow pond, are good sources for utilizing the waste and feeding the ducks.

TURTLES

Since turtles will eat plants and fish, they are not recommended for ponds. Although many types and sizes of turtles exist, most pond owners find that they are not an asset to pond life.

BIRDS

Some areas, such as ocean communities, have problems with predator birds. In order to protect your fish if predators are a problem, cover the pond with chicken wire or netting at approximately the 8-foot level, directly over the pond. Rubber snakes placed on the rocks or sides of the pond may also discourage predator birds.

RACCOONS/OPOSSUMS/ DOGS/CATS

Unfortunately, many potentially damaging animals may find their way to your pond. Some will stop for a drink of water, but most will eat the plants and fish and possibly tear up the structure of the pond itself. The only sure method of discouraging these visitors is an electric fence.

Among the animal packs themselves, such as with raccoons, the word gets around about the electric fence and soon deters them from the pond area. These thin wire fences will not destroy the aesthetic beauty of the pond.

HUMANS

Humans can be the pond's worst enemy. Problems in the pond can usually be traced back to the pond owner - too much interference. The pond gardener tends to prune the foliage too much, overfeed the fish, or put on boots and wade around, disturbing the natural biological action at the bottom of the pond.

Another aspect of human visitors to the pond is one that most beginners are unaware of and veterans are surprised about - some people are offensive about water gardens. Many of these people are simply ignorant about pond life and the balancing process, and others may question why your pond doesn't look like their swimming pool, a clear, sterile environment. Your best response is to take these comments in stride and go right on about your business of enjoying and appreciating nature at work in your water garden.

CHAPTER 8

Fountains And Waterfalls

FOUNTAINS & WATERFALLS

Hotel Shilla, Seoul, Korea.

Photo by Carolyn Uber.

Nothing points out the double-sided nature of a pond more than the addition of a fountain or waterfall. Take the normally quiet backyard pond, add a cascading waterfall and suddenly the pond is alive with sound and movement. The fact that a pond may have two distinct personalities doesn't mean, however, incompatibility. When constructed with a pump, both fountains and waterfalls can be turned on or off to achieve your desired effect.

Before adding a fountain or waterfall, be sure to consider your pond expectations. Do you want a quiet haven of relaxation, or are you looking for a dramatic, eye-catching focal point? Think about the type of sound you want to achieve – the rush of a running brook or the subtle sound of raindrops?

Waterfalls, cascades, sprays, and jets are the more ambitious and elaborate approaches to water gardening. Although fountains and waterfalls will create the visual and audio effects you may be looking for, they are not essential to the pond's well-being.

Neither fountains nor waterfalls should be constructed as lifetime, permanent fixtures. Not only should a pond be recognized as an ever-changing source of beauty, but from the practical side, constantly running water eventually creates a calcium and mineral buildup. When constructed as an addition to the pond, fountains and waterfalls are two features that can be updated, changed, or remodeled at some later date.

FOUNTAINS

For centuries Europeans have enjoyed the beauty of fountains in their public squares and private gardens. Many famous fountains have occurred in nature, yet other man-made fountains have been with us for centuries. In Ancient Greece and Rome, fountains were scattered throughout the countryside so people could draw household water.

Today, in modern architecture fountains are again taking their place as an art form in many city parks, plazas and buildings. Some of these new public fountains are patterned after ancient water hydraulic systems, while others, in keeping with new technology, are operated by solar cell pumps.

Homeowners, too, can enjoy the beauty of a fountain. Even the smallest patio or yard

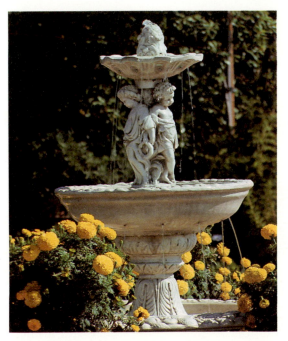

Custom-made, multi-tiered, statuary fountains and other supplies are available through water garden suppliers. Photos by Carolyn Uber.

can accommodate a small fountain. Rather than playing a dominant role in the formal garden as in years gone by, most of today's fountains are integrated into the overall water garden design.

Fountainheads may be installed in an existing pond for an added dimension, yet a pond isn't necessary for the creation of a fountain. Almost any water-holding container will accommodate the required essentials. Half wine barrels are popular with many water gardeners, or an arrangement of three barrels and a fountainhead, with water cascading from one barrel to another, creates a fountain/waterfall look.

Simple fountains consist of a single jet of water; others feature a mass of sprays. Some fountainheads rotate, while others change the water patterns. Fountainheads and fountain kits, which may be purchased from water garden suppliers, will vary in prices, from just a few dollars up to several thousand. Sprinkler heads and pulsating shower heads can also serve as fountains.

How to Install
Fountains may be installed by several methods, both with and without pumps.

Two types of pumps, which continually recycle the same water, are available: the exterior, self-priming pump or the submersible pump. The most commonly used pump is the submersible one, which is easier to install and inexpensive to run. Place the pump near the bottom of the pond. Run the electrical line to an outside electrical box with a ground fault interrupter (GFI).

Fountains may be installed in three ways:

1. FOUNTAIN BASIN - These custom-made, multi-tier, statuary fountains are available through water garden suppliers. Using a shim where necessary helps to keep the unit level, since most ponds are not entirely level on the bottom. A built-in water valve regulates the amount of water flowing through the fountainhead.

2. FOUNTAINHEAD ADJUSTABLE BASE - Although expensive, this sturdy, self-sustaining unit has three adjustable legs. A fountainhead attaches to the top and a water valve regulates the water flow.

3. STUBBED-IN FOUNTAINS - The pump lines can either be stubbed-in through the cement, following the instructions in Chapter Two under "Building the Pond - Submersible Pump," or water lines, weighted down with a cement brick or sand bag, can be run across the bottom of the pond.

The fountainhead should be installed slightly above the surface of the water to achieve the full effect of the spray pattern. A gate valve for regulating the flow of water is a useful addition. Make certain that the spray of the fountain doesn't go over the edge of the pond, or hit plant foliage. The pond dimensions should be approximately twice the height of a single spout fountain jet.

Pre-fabricated fountain kits come in different sizes and various types of sprays. *Photo by Clint Bryant.*

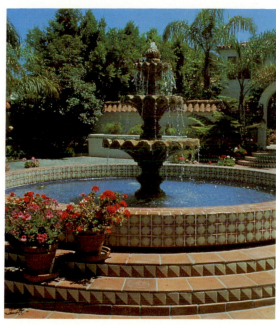

Opposite, Top Left: The statuary fountain at the Claremont Colleges, California, offers a refreshing attraction to students and visitors alike.   Photo by Dennis Tannen.
Opposite, Top Right: Dramatic waterfalls can be created in narrow areas, such as this one in Tokyo, Japan.
                    Photo by Carolyn Uber.
Opposite, Bottom Left: Waterfalls are one of nature's -- and man's -- most beautiful creations. New Otani Hotel, Tokyo, Japan.   Photo by Carolyn Uber.
Opposite, Bottom Right: Night lighting creates a special effect on fountains and waterfalls.
            Photo by Dennis Tannen

Above: The tiled, statuary fountain at the Langslet residence in Belmont Shores, California offers an "old world" look.
            Photo courtesy of Lifescapes, Inc.
Top, Right: Night lighting around this fountain ring produces a dramatic, eye-catching effect.
              Photo by Dennis Tannen.
Right: Decorative water gardening is as practical for homeowners as it is for professional landscapers and architects.
        Photo courtesy of DiGiacomo, Inc.

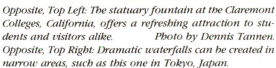

FOUNTAINS & WATERFALLS

PVC pipe is usually recommended, since it is easy to work with. The vibration of a rotating head occasionally causes the fountain to wobble; therefore, you may be wise to steady the PVC pipe with rocks or bricks. If you use rigid PVC, use electrical 90's to reduce back pressure on the pump.

Some fountainheads, such as rotating heads or those with small holes, will clog easily, so a filter may be necessary. Micron filters are especially effective in filtering out minute particles without affecting the elements, compounds or chemicals in the pond.

Algae clings to statuary-type fountains, and although most water gardeners like the natural look, others may not. If you don't like the natural look of algae, shut the

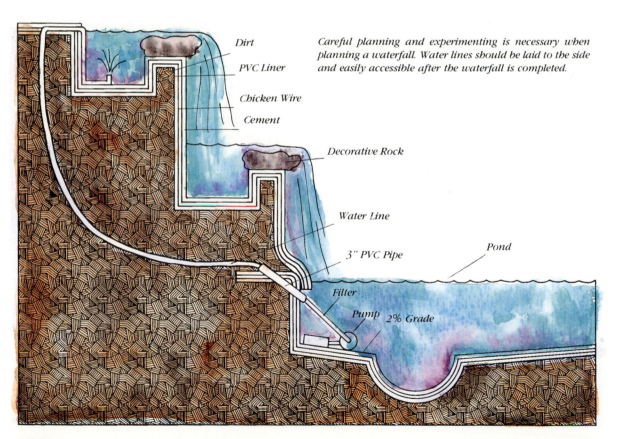

Dirt

PVC Liner

Chicken Wire

Cement

Decorative Rock

Water Line

3" PVC Pipe

Pond

Filter

Pump

2% Grade

Careful planning and experimenting is necessary when planning a waterfall. Water lines should be laid to the side and easily accessible after the waterfall is completed.

fountain off during the morning hours each day to burn the algae off. Black or solid color PVC tubing for the water lines, rather than clear tubing, also deters algae growth.

WATERFALLS

Waterfalls are one of nature's most beautiful creations, and one that the average water gardener can re-create in the backyard pond by using some foresight and planning. Waterfalls add another dimension to your pond, whether it be a dramatic, cascading waterfall or the gentle flow of a mountain stream.

Careful planning and experimenting is essential in order to build a waterfall that appears natural. The scope for the design of

Left: This natural-looking waterfall complements the lush green landscaping in the aviary at the Los Angeles Zoo. Photo courtesy of DiGiacomo, Inc.
Right: The pond at The Arbors townhomes in Fullerton, California, demonstrates that the scope of designs using water are unlimited.   Photo courtesy of Lifescapes, Inc.

waterfalls in unlimited. Water receptacles, arranged one above the other, can be made with a variety of materials – rocks, concrete basins, wooden frames, and even bowls or buckets.

A waterfall should not have more water capacity than the pond can accommodate when the waterfall is not running. The base pond should be at least four times the size of the waterfall.

Pump Capabilities

Three types of pumps may be used when constructing a waterfall. Since the most visually pleasing ponds have water which is circulated once per hour, read the various manufacturer's performance charts and instructions in order to check each pump's capabilities.

SUBMERSIBLE PUMPS - These noise-free pumps are inexpensive to operate and easy to install. Waterfalls that require a considerable amount of water may use several submersible pumps as opposed to one large pump.

EXTERIOR SELF-PRIMING PUMPS - This type of pump operates outside the pond, requires 220 electrical wiring, and should be housed off the ground on a cement slab in a weatherproof chamber.

FOUNTAINS & WATERFALLS

Left: Low, wide waterfalls can be just as effective as tall, dramatic ones.   Photo by Carolyn Uber.
Right: Waterfall sounds can be amplified with rocks jutting out from the structure of the waterfall leaving a hollow space behind the falling water.   Photo by Carolyn Uber.

Recreational facilities at Val Vista Lakes, Arizona, include three large lakes and this waterfall swimming lagoon. Photo courtesy of Lifescapes, Inc.

Since these pumps have the capability of using sand filters, skimmers, vacuums and air jets, they are commonly used in commercial installations and koi ponds where balancing may be a problem.

SUMP PUMP - Although sump pumps are not designed for filters, they may be used for waterfalls. The low price makes a sump pump attractive to many gardeners. However, it usually is not recommended since it uses a great deal of electricity and has no back pressure capabilities.

Determining the Amount of Water

One of the first major considerations is to determine how much water will be necessary to achieve the right waterfall look. You'll need to do a lot of experimenting with your garden hose. Turn the water on and hold the hose at different heights and in different areas of the pond. Prop the hose up at a height you find pleasing and let the water run.

Now test the sound your waterfall makes. Walk around the yard, the house, your bedroom, and even your neighbor's yard and listen. Experiment by turning the water flow up and down until you achieve the desired effect, both audio and visual.

Estimating Water Quantity

Once you achieve the desired effect, you'll have to calculate the number of gallons of water per hour, using the following method:
Run the hose at the desired rate, filling a one-gallon can and timing it in seconds. For

example, if it takes 10 seconds to fill a gallon, and there are 60 seconds in a minute, your waterfall takes 6 gallons a minute or 360 gallons per hour.

Height is the second factor to consider since pumps are rated by gallons per hour at certain heights. Measure the distance from where the pump will sit, either in the pond or out, to the highest point of the waterfall.

The pump should be as near the waterfall as possible for adequate circulation. If not, make the following adjustments: With a long lateral line, reduce the water pressure total by 10-percent for each 10-foot increment of lateral line. Solid or black flexible vinyl tubing should be used wherever possible. However, if you use rigid PVC, then use electrical 90's and if you use a standard 90, it will reduce your water pressure by 20-percent from the total for each standard 90.

Planning How the Water Falls

The backdrop to a waterfall can be almost anything, even dirt left over from digging the pond. If you use dirt, be sure to tamp it well and run a sprinkler overnight for proper packing. Existing walls, 55-gallon drums, or old cement blocks can also serve as backdrops.

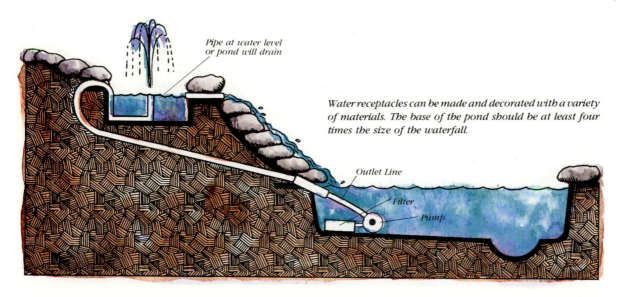

Pipe at water level or pond will drain

Water receptacles can be made and decorated with a variety of materials. The base of the pond should be at least four times the size of the waterfall.

Outlet Line

Filter

Pump

FOUNTAINS & WATERFALLS

Once you've determined the height and waterfall location, the next step is planning the water's pathway. If you want the water to gently run down your waterfall, beveling the dirt in a manner you like is all that is required. However, if you want the water to fall one or more times, more experimenting will be necessary.

Get some large bowls, pans or 5-gallon buckets, then turn the hose to the desired amount of water. Using these different diameter containers, place the hose inside and watch how the water flows off. If you want the water to fall from a rock lip, hold the rock to the edge of the various containers and watch the way the water runs off. The rock size or the container angle may have to be changed to achieve the right effect. A great deal of trial and error may be required before producing a waterfall that is satisfying.

Constructing the Waterfall

Because waterfalls are alternately wet and dry, the cement, rocks, wood and other construction materials continually expand and contract. For this reason the base of the

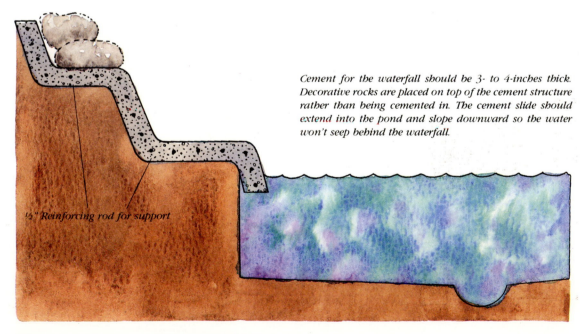

Cement for the waterfall should be 3- to 4-inches thick. Decorative rocks are placed on top of the cement structure rather than being cemented in. The cement slide should extend into the pond and slope downward so the water won't seep behind the waterfall.

½" Reinforcing rod for support

waterfall is the most important consideration in construction and unfortunately the most neglected. Water will slide down the fall in two ways:

- *the visual water that runs down the exterior waterfall, and*
- *the water that seeps down the cracks below the waterfall.*

The water lines should be laid to the side and easily accessible after the waterfall is completed. Use a PVC threaded fitting, one size larger than the feed line, at the top of the waterfall and cement it in with both ends exposed. (The fitting can always be reduced later.) The end of the water line which is in the waterfall should be placed in a basin at least 4-inches deep so the pressure will not spray, but rather will mulch.

Bevel the cement slide toward the center and slope towards the pond. (Cross Section)

(Should you desire a spray, experiment with the threaded end.)

Following are two construction methods for your waterfall footing:

CEMENT FOOTING - The cement must be 3- to 4-inches thick, with a 1/2-inch rebar every 12-inches on center and #3 wire on top. Place the rebar 2-inches off the ground or in the center of the cement. Lay the cement one-foot on either side of the waterfall, beveling toward the center and sloping toward the pond. The most critical portion of the waterslide is at the joint with the pond. The rebar and cement must extend into the pond and slope downward so the water won't seep behind the waterfall into the dirt.

PVC LINED FOOTING - The easiest and least expensive method for constructing the waterfall is PVC liner. (Use PVC only, since poly sheeting will neither work nor last.) Allow plenty of PVC lining material so you can fold and tuck as necessary. Lay the PVC liner in the beveled area, extending at least one-foot on either side of the waterfall and sloping toward the pond. Again, the most important section is the joint of the pond and liner. Be sure to extend the liner into

FOUNTAINS & WATERFALLS

the pond and tar between the liner and pond.

Once the PVC liner is in place, cover it with chicken wire. The chicken wire is the structure for the cement. If you are using a cement slab, nail the chicken wire down in a few places along the sides, taking care not to break the edge of the slab.

Once you've artistically set the rocks, wood or other decorative items into place, you can begin cementing. Following is the cement mix:

- *1 shovel cement*
- *4 shovels sand*
- *1/4 gallon fire clay per 15 shovels of mix*
- *Dye, if desired*

Using the information you obtained from your bowl and bucket experiment, you can now begin developing your waterfall. If you so desire, use the old bowls and buckets for the waterfall basins rather than forming them by hand. Falls will make more noise if some of the rocks jut out with a hollow space behind the falling water.

You can spend as much time as necessary constructing your PVC-lined or cement waterfall since cracks are not a problem with the waterslide. If you are unhappy with the way the water falls, you can easily knock out a section and redo it, taking care not to damage the PVC or the cement slide.

Trim the liner after all the cementing is complete and you are satisfied with the looks and sounds.

TIMERS/LIGHTING/ELECTRICITY

Timers may be used to turn the pumps on and off. Small pumps may be run all day, while large pumps should only run four to six hours a day.

Lighting the waterfall or fountain is mostly personal choice. However, lighting under the waterfall tends to produce a harsh look. A series of 12-volt exterior lights, accenting the waterfall or fountain, offers a softer look.

Building codes require that lights be attached to an outside J Box with a ground fault interrupter (GFI) and be located 5-feet away from the pond. Check with your local Planning Department for other electrical regulations.

CHAPTER 9

Pond Maintenance

Hotel/Shopping Center Complex. *Photo by Dennis Tannen.*

CLEANING THE POND

TIMING - With proper preparation and planning, the actual cleaning process shouldn't take long, depending on the pond size. Your most important consideration will be to work quickly and efficiently to get the fish back into the pond before they die or become overly stressed.

The ideal temperature for pond cleaning is 50 to 70 degrees, with cloud cover and possibly a little moisture.

PREPARATION - Preparation for pond cleaning is extremely important. Assemble the following supplies before you begin:

- *Pump*
- *Hose*
- *Toilet brush or stiff broom*
- *Boots or tennis shoes*
- *Wading pool to hold fish*
- *Shovel*
- *Nozzle*
- *Bucket (5-gallon)*
- *Bucket (1-gallon)*
- *Net*
- *Fertilizer*
- *2 x 8 x 12-foot plank*
- *Setup Chemicals*

ORGANIZATION - Organization is another important factor in pond cleaning. The following suggested steps will help you organize your project:

- *Set up fish holding tank*
- *Drain pond to 2-inches* (In

chloramine areas, you may wish to save the pond water in holding tanks.)
- *Remove fish*
- *Remove plants* (Only if replanting, otherwise work around the plants, keeping them moist.)
- *Rinse Pond*
- *Refill pond and use setup chemicals*
- *Put fish back into pond*
- *Take a break*
- *Remove and rinse snails*
- *Clean, replant, fertilize plants*
- *Place plants in pond*
- *Clean area around pond*
- *Follow setup charts for 60-days*

Setting up Fish Tanks

Fish, like all other animals, have to breathe. Displaced fish need a large surface area with shallow water. A child's wading pool, with its large surface, is one of the best holding tanks. Trash cans, as another example, are not good holding tanks. They provide a large volume of water, but only a small surface area. Without enough surface area, your fish can literally die or become severely stressed in an improper holding tank.

Allow one-square foot of surface area for each 5-inches of fish in the holding tank.

MAINTENANCE

Fish are measured from their mouth to the end of their caudal fin (tail fin).

Shade is another important consideration. Your fish should be kept cool at all times. Good areas to set up a temporary pond are under a tree, or in a garage or patio.

Depending on the temperature and water quality, the fish should not remain in the temporary pond any longer than one- to two-hours. If the fish begin gapping, they must be returned to the pond, or immediately aerate the temporary pond with a pump.

If your pond cleaning and/or repairing will take longer than two-hours, your bathtub may be used as a fish tank. Empty and refresh 25-percent of the water twice a day. Fish may be fed while they are housed in the bathtub.

Fill the temporary holding tank with about 6- to 8-inches of water taken from the middle of the pond. In order to fill the holding tank, you may need to set the pump up on a bucket or lily pot. The fish holding tank should be filled no sooner than 30 minutes before removing the fish. Old water tends to lose oxygen.

Treat the temporary holding tank with salt and vitamins (1/4-lb. formulated fish salt per 25-gallons of water and 3 drops of liquid vitamins per 100-gallons of water).

If you have an extra pump, set it in the tank with the outlet head 2-inches below the water surface area. Using a pump will create a mulching effect and fill the water with oxygen to help the fish breathe. Make certain the pump has a strainer so the fish won't get stuck in the inlet.

Drain Pond to 2-Inches

Drain the pond to 2-inches of water. If your pond is large, you may want to place wet papers or cloths on the plants to prevent sunburn. Wet them down occasionally to keep healthy. The frequency of wetting down will depend on the temperature; the hotter it is, the more you will cool them off.

Fill a 5-gallon bucket with clean pond water and place it in a shady spot for use when removing the fish. Fill the 1-gallon bucket with pond water for rinsing your snails later.

Removing Fish

Do not get into the pond unless absolutely necessary. If it should become necessary to get into the pond, wear water boots or old tennis shoes to prevent slipping.

With the pond at 2-inches of water,

142

begin catching the fish with your net, taking care not to injure them. When you spot a fish, place the front of the net on the bottom, holding it at a 45-degree angle. With your other hand, reach under the fish and carefully shove the fish into the net, making sure not to scrape the fish on the pond bottom.

Place the fish into the 5-gallon bucket you filled earlier and transport to the holding tank. Use calm, easy movements and keep your voice low. Loud noises and hurried movements will frighten the fish into injuring themselves. Don't delay at this point, and don't concern yourself about the snails.

Watch the fish, making sure they don't start gapping for air at the top of the holding tank. If they begin gapping, periodically mulch the water with your hands. Time is now critical for fish health.

Removing Plants

After your fish have been removed from the pond, begin removing all plants that are to be replanted to an area near the pond; otherwise leave them in the pond, working around them and making sure they are moist at all times. Don't attempt to move the plants any great distance since they are saturated with water and may be heavy. Overgrown plants should be cut into easy-

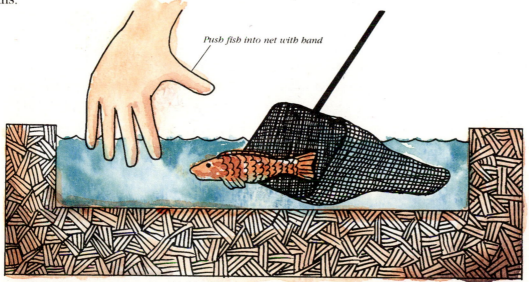

Push fish into net with hand

With the pond at 2-inches of water, carefully direct fish into the net while holding it at a 45-degree angle.

Heavy aquatic plant pots can be removed from the pond by using a 2x8 plank to slide them up and out.

to-handle sections. If possible, two people should lift the plants out. One suggestion for removing the plants is to use a 2 x 8 plank to slide the pots up and out.

Based on each plant's survival time outside of the pond, remove the plants in the following order: 1) oxygenating grasses (collect all you can and keep them wet while they're outside of the pond), 2) water lilies, 3) small flowering ornamentals, and 4) bog plants.

Rinsing the Pond

With a broom and shovel, sweep and scoop the water and dirt out of the pond. Don't haul the dirt away now. Not only will it be messy, but time is of the essence and it will be easier to handle when dry. Place the dirt and water in a flower bed or on the lawn. Nutrients from the dirt and water will help your plants, and the salts are not a problem.

When most of the dirt and water are removed, take a high pressure nozzle and

144

spray down the sides and/or waterfall, and clean any water lines to the waterfall or fountain. Do not remove or damage the slime on the sides of your pond. The high pressure nozzle will simply remove excess algae. Keep the slime moist during the pond cleaning. If you have hair algae that wasn't removed by the spraying nozzle, use a stiff broom or a new, clean toilet brush to brush it off. Don't remove all this algae; the fish will eat the residue pieces.

Rinse the pond again, leaving some of the bottom waste. The hard waste left on the bottom will help re-establish a new biological waste center.

Once the pond is rinsed, begin filling with fresh water immediately. Put in the pond setup chemicals, following the setup chart shown in Chapter Three. Thoroughly mix all chemicals. If you have chloramines, be sure to use a chloramine reducer. When adding a solid reducer, place it in a stocking and run the hose over it until the pond is full. Dump any residue into the pond, and wait an extra 30 to 90 minutes before re-establishing the fish.

Snails

Begin collecting all the snails you can find. Using a colander, rinse them lightly in the 1-gallon bucket of pond water. (Fresh water may have chloramines that will kill the snails.) Return the snails to the pond in a corner you are not likely to step in. These snails will live for about 10 days, during

Water Snails do not leave the pond. They live, eat, and reproduce within the confines of the pond structure. Neither will they overrun the pond. In a balanced pond, snails will balance themselves out.

145

which time they will lay eggs, and from these eggs will come a new group of snails. Don't trim new plants in your clean pond for at least a month, since they may shelter snail eggs.

Returning the Fish to the Pond

Once the pond is filled, begin floating the fish back in the pond. Fish can be floated back in buckets, plastic bags or trash cans. Float for 20 minutes. This floating process will help equalize the water temperatures so as not to shock the fish. For that reason, metal buckets or trash cans are preferable over plastic. However, if you do not have metal, use plastic rather than hold up the process of getting the fish back into the pond.

Break Time

While your fish are acclimating to the pond, it's a good time to take a 10 to 30 minute break. Your fish are safe and the plants will hold.

Replanting and Refertilizing

Complete planting instructions for water plants may be found in Chapter Four. Following are simple instructions:

OXYGENATING GRASSES - Rinse the grasses lightly, separating into the number of grass pots needed for your pond, or one pot per 100-gallons of water. Repot with new soil unless the plants have good roots. Return these plants to the pond.

WATER LILIES - Inspect your lilies before returning them to the pond. A 3-year-old water lily will out-bloom a new plant. Flowers are the plants' means of survival. When a plant is root bound, it will start to flower.

Most of your plants can be re-established with a little dirt and fertilizer. Replant at least 10-percent of the pots, but no more than 50-percent.

SMALL FLOWERING ORNAMENTALS - All ornamentals should be replanted.

BOG PLANTS- Take your shovel and cut a section of the bog equal to 1/3 of its pot. Place fertilizer on the bottom of the pot, put a chunk of the bog in the center, and pack the soil around it. Trim the foliage to 6-inches from the top of the pot and return the plant to the pond.

Cleaning the Area Around the Pond

Wash all dirt off the cement to prevent staining. If you leave the dirt and plant material on the lawn for about a week, it will dry enough for easy removal. This material is excellent for gardens or planters when mixed half and half with soil.

Removing Stains

Stains can usually be removed from cement areas by using a light solution of Clorox® and water. Be careful of your clothes, and be sure the Clorox® doesn't get into the pond. Any stains on your hands can also be removed by using a light solution of Clorox® and water, then rinse thoroughly. Don't use Clorox® on wood or paint, or other products that will stain.

Following Through

All of your pond cleaning work could very well be wasted if you don't follow up with your pond setup chemicals. The control of algae while your plants re-establish themselves is most important. Using the Salt and Vitamin Treatments as mentioned in Chapter Six will keep your fish healthy.

SEASONAL POND MAINTENANCE

If you're spending more than 15 minutes per month per thousand gallons of water, you're spending too much time on your pond. A balanced pond requires minimal seasonal maintenance.

Spring Maintenance

Not only is spring a good time for building a pond, but it's also the ideal time for cleaning. Once the plants start budding, it's time to vacuum the bottom or clean the pond and get rid of decayed vegetation. However, this should be done with care, not by devastating the pond. Remove no more than 25-percent of the overgrown grasses and plants no oftener than every two weeks. Follow the instructions in Chapter Four and Chapter Five for re-potting your plants.

You can expect a certain amount of green water algae in the spring when the weather warms and the pond activity begins speeding up after the dormant winter months. This green water condition should clear itself up after a short period of time, usually about two weeks.

During late spring when the plants have tender new growth, they may need protection from aphids and cutworms. One method is a nightly, light washing with an overhead sprinkler. (Daytime watering may sunburn the plants.) Another method is to use a 5-percent solution of Ortho's Volck Supreme Oil Spray and spray all foliage in and near the pond. It will not harm the fish or plants.

Summer Maintenance

Maintain a monthly pruning schedule

MAINTENANCE

during the summer months, removing only the brown or yellowed leaves. Cut the center leaves out of the plants so the plants can take in more sunlight. Take care not to remove all the snail eggs, which are detectable as the clear jelly substance attached to the underside of the water lily leaves. Again, in order not to greatly disturb your pond's balance, go slowly in removing plants or foliage.

Summer is also an ideal time to feed existing plants and add new varieties.

Fall Maintenance

In mild climates, fall is another good time to clean the pond, or at the minimum, keep all dead foliage pruned. Watch for pests, aphids and cutworms. Spray again, if necessary.

Winter Maintenance

During the winter months the fish become less and less active and the plants become dormant. Dormancy is triggered when the water cools down. The water lilies then begin devoting their energies and resources to the tuber. Blooming stops and leaf size diminishes.

In moderate climates, little is required for maintaining the pond through the winter months. However, freezing climates may cause problems for some water gardeners. If the pond's freezing level goes down to the plants' roots, remove only the water lilies, bogs, and small flowering aquatics. The oxygenating grasses and fish may remain in the pond. Cover the pond with fiberglass as protection for your fish, or a horse trough set up under cover makes a satisfactory home for fish.

In order to leave their plants in the pond during the winter months, some pond gardeners use heaters, while others make fiberglass covers for their ponds. A structure of 2 x 4 planks, laid across the pond and covered with fiberglass sheeting, will act as an insulator. It's important to keep the fiberglass panel 4- to 6-inches above the water surface so the pond can breathe.

Placing one or more logs in the water, depending on the pond size, also helps prevent heavy ice from forming and keeps the cement from cracking.

With the exception of tropical water lilies, aquatic plants can be moved to the basement and stored in their pots in sealed trash bags or covered with wet cloths during the freezing weeks. These plants should be kept moist at all times. Around February begin sprouting the water plants in a greenhouse or other warm area.

In frost-free areas, tropical water lilies are best left in the year around. In colder climates, they can be removed for the winter by following these steps:

- *After the first frost, remove the water lily, container and all, to a cool, dark area and cover with a wet cloth. Let the bulb sit for 15 days (this forces carbohydrates into the bulb).*
- *Remove the bulb from the pot, rinse and place in a tub of water for two weeks. Rinse the bulbs daily.*
- *Pack the bulb in a sealed container such as a glass jar or plastic bag. Fill the container with 1-inch of damp sand, add the bulb and pack additional sand to the top. Seal the container and label. Store in a cool, dark area 55 to 65 degrees. (The sand for the bulb should be just damp. If it's too wet, the bulb will rot; if it's too dry, the bulb will dry out. Fill a perforated container with sand, wet down and allow it to drain for 24 hours. The sand will be ready to use.)*

- *One month before the warm weather, begin sprouting the bulb. Place it in a small container of water in a greenhouse or sunny window. When the weather turns to 70 degrees, repot 1/4-inch below fresh soil and fertilizer mixture. Place the pot 4- to 6-inches below the water.*

The pond at this West Germany botanical garden is heated during the winter in order to keep the Tropical water lilies blooming year round.   Photo by Carolyn Uber.

MAINTENANCE

MAINTENANCE CHART

To keep your pond looking its best — and plants and fish healthy,
follow this monthly maintenance program. Use this handy
checklist each month as a reminder.

☐	☐	☐	☐	☐	☐	☐	☐	☐	☐	☐	☐	☐	☐	☐	☐	☐	JANUARY
☐	☐	☐	☐	☐	☐	☐	☐	☐	☐	☐	☐	☐	☐	☐	☐	☐	FEBRUARY
☐	☐	☐	☐	☐	☐	☐	☐	☐	☐	☐	☐	☐	☐	☐	☐	☐	MARCH
☐	☐	☐	☐	☐	☐	☐	☐	☐	☐	☐	☐	☐	☐	☐	☐	☐	APRIL
☐	☐	☐	☐	☐	☐	☐	☐	☐	☐	☐	☐	☐	☐	☐	☐	☐	MAY
☐	☐	☐	☐	☐	☐	☐	☐	☐	☐	☐	☐	☐	☐	☐	☐	☐	JUNE
☐	☐	☐	☐	☐	☐	☐	☐	☐	☐	☐	☐	☐	☐	☐	☐	☐	JULY
☐	☐	☐	☐	☐	☐	☐	☐	☐	☐	☐	☐	☐	☐	☐	☐	☐	AUGUST
☐	☐	☐	☐	☐	☐	☐	☐	☐	☐	☐	☐	☐	☐	☐	☐	☐	SEPTEMBER
☐	☐	☐	☐	☐	☐	☐	☐	☐	☐	☐	☐	☐	☐	☐	☐	☐	OCTOBER
☐	☐	☐	☐	☐	☐	☐	☐	☐	☐	☐	☐	☐	☐	☐	☐	☐	NOVEMBER
☐	☐	☐	☐	☐	☐	☐	☐	☐	☐	☐	☐	☐	☐	☐	☐	☐	DECEMBER

1. Remove old foliage
2. Add soil to pots as needed
3. Replant pots as required
4. Remove small plants from lily root
5. Fertilize with tablets
6. Sweep pond bottom
7. Inspect fish for diseases
8. Spray pool for aphids
9. Use algae control chemical
10. Clean filter and pressurize pump lines
11. Protect tropical bulbs with ½" wire cage
12. Inspect pond for cracks and patch as necessary
13. Check GFI ground
14. Feed fish
15. Note plants required and replace
16. Test water for ammonia
17. Check pH (range 7.5 - 9.5)

Other Water Gardens

OTHER GARDENS

Avery International, Pasadena, California.   *Photo courtesy of DiGiacomo, Inc.*

NATURAL CREEKS
OR STREAMS

While most areas of the world give every indication of being overpopulated and industrialized, a few folks are fortunate enough to live alongside the edge of a river, while still others have natural creeks or streams flowing through their properties. Although having access to these natural bodies of water may seem to give the prospective gardener a head start on developing a garden pond, the truth is that these natural waters are usually too cold for water plants to grow well. However, with some foresight and planning these natural environments can be converted into beautiful water gardens.

Water temperature is the most crucial aspect in working with the natural creek or stream. Before constructing your water garden, measure the water temperature at various times of the day and during the different seasons. (Some streams drop 30 degrees or more during the winter months.) Water plants grow best in 65 to 70 degree water. For each degree below these optimum conditions there is a marked difference in the plant's growing

Some of nature's most fascinating water gardens are creeks and streams that follow the course Nature has set out for them.

capabilities. Even in streams with temperatures of 65 degrees and below, a variety of techniques can be used to warm up the water.

One technique is to build a pond within the stream, placing the water garden portion away from the main current of water. This garden area should remain relatively quiet and warm, the ideal setting for a waterscape.

Diverting a portion of the stream to run over black PVC, or through corrugated pipe which has been painted black, is another technique for warming the water. The darker the color of the heat-conducting

Tub gardens are adaptable to almost any size or type of container, including caldrons, wooden tubs, crock pots, wash tubs, and even old bathtubs.
Photos by Dennis Tannen.

material, the more heat will be generated. Also for optimum warming conditions, the pond should be 18- to 24-inches deep.

If the water tempertaure stays within the 65 to 70 degree range, plant tropical water lilies; otherwise, hardy water lilies will thrive better in the cooler waters. Once your pond is established, the continuing overflow of stream water will keep the pond clear and healthy.

Some aquatic plants that grow well along the sides of a warm area of the creek or stream include such bog plants as azure pickerel, arrowhead, equisetum or umbrella palm. Other types of aquatics include parrot's feather, pennywort, primrose creeper and water hyacinth.

TUB GARDENS

Tub gardens deserve a category for themselves. They are not quite large enough in size to reach the maturity of a water garden, yet, they are popular and attractive forms of water gardening, both indoors and out.

A small tub garden is an excellent way to introduce children to the world of water gardening. Many youngsters learn all about ocean tide pools, seaweed, and starfish, but they know little about this backyard form of gardening with aquatic plants and small creatures. Tub gardens are so simple that children can easily plant and care for one of their own.

Indoor Tub Garden

An indoor tub garden may be constructed in the following manner:

- *Select a half-gallon size, or larger, container jar.*
- *If you desire, place a small amount of soil on the bottom, although soil is not absolutely necessary to the garden's success. Sand and fertilizer tablets work well in maintaining the indoor tub garden.*
- *Plant the container with bog plants, oxygenating grasses and/or small flowering ornamentals and place the container in a window, preferably with a southern exposure.*
- *Mosquito fish are recommended for the indoor tub garden.*
- *Aquarium nutrient tablets will aid in the control of algae. If plants begin turning yellow, they probably need extra nitrogen.*

Outdoor Tub Garden

Tub gardens are the perfect answer for small space gardening. They may be created in the space it takes to put a large planter or barbeque grill. Tub gardens are perfect for apartments, condominium patios or balconies and mobile homes as well as beautifying areas in large yards.

Select any size or type of container that suits your location, although to avoid problems in gas exchanges, a tub garden should be no deeper than 18-inches. Tub gardens are adaptable to wooden tubs, wash tubs, crock pots, old bathtubs and even horse troughs. Olive, wine or whiskey barrels can be used if they are lined with PVC to protect the fish and plants from harmful bacteria that may have been left from the fermenting process.

Tub gardens are easy to install, and they don't require pumps, filters, drains or chemicals. However, if desired, a small fountain can make an attractive addition.

Location is probably the most important consideration. The ideal location is level, sunny and not too close to deciduous trees and shrubs. Since tub gardens are susceptible to temperature changes, place your tub on rollers, so it can

OTHER GARDENS

Tub gardens are the perfect answer for small space gardening -- apartments, condominium patios, balconies or mobile homes. They may be created in the space it takes to put a large planter or barbeque grill.

be moved as the sun changes during the day. Once filled with soil and water, tubs are too heavy to be moved. Three to four hours of direct or indirect sunlight are usually sufficient, preferably during the early morning or late afternoon hours rather than during the heat of the day.

Visual concept is another aspect when considering location. Since most people

enjoy the beauty of their water gardens while sitting, don't place the container too high or above eye level while seated. Tub gardens can also be sunk into the ground.

The quantity and types of plants will vary with your desired landscaping effect and the size of your container. The same clear water formula recommended in Chapter Three applies to the tub garden. For each square yard of surface area, you should have:

- *Two bunches oxygenating grasses*
- *One medium to large water lily*
- *Twelve water snails*
- *Guppie or mosquito fish*

WATER PLANTS - Oxygenating grasses absorb carbon dioxide and replenish oxygen, thereby helping with the control of algae. Water lilies provide surface coverage which prevents oxygen loss and keeps the water cooler during the warm months. During the winter months, the aquatic plants will go dormant.

SNAILS - Water snails assume the same role in the tub garden as they do in the large pond. They are the algae scavengers of the garden, neither leaving the tub nor eating the decorative plants.

FISH - Goldfish and koi are not recommended for tub gardens since they are sensitive to fluctuations in temperatures and gas exchanges. Mosquito fish or guppies are generally suggested.

Tub gardens are easy to plant:

- *Fill the container 1/4-full of sandy loam.*
- *Add correct amount of aquatic plant fertilizer for the volume of soil.*
- *Fill container to halfway mark with soil.*
- *Cover with 1/4-inch sand.*
- *Place an old sock over the end of the hose and slowly fill the container with 1-inch of water without disturbing the soil.*
- *Plant the water lily at a 45-degree angle in the middle of the tub with bogs and grasses planted around the outer edges.* (Plants can also be planted in containers, following the instructions for planting in Chapter Four, and stacked on rocks at appropriate depths in the water.)
- *Slowly fill water to the top.*
- *Float the fish in the the same plastic containers you brought them home*

With foresight and planning, natural environments can be converted into beautiful water gardens.

in for 20 to 40 minutes before releasing them into the tub garden.

Wine, whiskey and olive casks should be lined with PVC sheeting. To determine the amount of PVC sheeting required, multiply the container's depth by two. Add this number to the sum of the pool's maximum width and length. For a 12-inch overlap on each side include an additional 2-feet of liner.

OTHER GARDENS

Attaining proper balance in your tub garden is your first priority and it is a simple task if you basically let nature take its course. Tub gardens thrive on neglect! Your tub garden should not be crystal clear like a swimming pool. Small amounts of floating and clinging algae are necessary as food for fish and nutrients for water plants.

Garden balance is usually achieved within 30 to 60 days without chemical controls. In the beginning balance is best achieved by trickling small amounts of water into the tub garden for about 30 days. This minute amount of chlorine will control algae until the garden is balanced.

Too much algae probably indicates insufficient sunlight or too many nutrients. The problem can be prevented by giving the tub garden more sunlight or by pruning excess or old foliage and removing fallen leaves and twigs.

Prices for tub gardens will vary according to your desires. Most water garden suppliers offer kits for the beginner which include a tub, tropical water lily, bog plant, and one bunch of oxygenating grasses.

The following varieties of aquatic plants are particularly well-suited to tub garden life:

Grasses - *Anacharis, Cabomba, Miniature sagittaria, Myriophyllum,* and *Vallisneria.*

Day-Blooming Tropical Water Lilies - *Midnight, Tina, Mrs. Martin E. Randig, Pink Capensis, Dauben, Jack Wood, Pennsylvania, Zanzibar Blue, Director Moore,* and *St. Louis Gold.*

Night-Blooming Tropical Water Lilies - *Mrs. John A. Wood, Sir Galahad,* and *Rosa de Noche.*

Hardy Water Lilies - *Marliac Carnea, Odorata sulfuria, Paul Hariot, Attraction, Gladstoniana, Marliacea chromatella,* and *Pygmae helvola.*

BOG GARDENS

The moisture-loving bog plants described in Chapter Four can be transformed into a beautiful garden all their own. A bog garden can be constructed alongside your water garden and designed as part of the overall effect, or it can be used as a separate landscaping technique.

Wet or Dry Areas

In problem areas where nothing will grow because of the heat, a bog garden may be the answer. Since a bog garden thrives on heavy moisture, many dry areas can be developed into lush green oases. Conversely, those areas that remain constantly wet the year-round can be beautified by creating a bog garden.

Unique Design

Bog plants create their own unique patterns and designs, whether it be the graceful cattail or the stately umbrella palm. The possibilities in design for a bog garden are varied. By planting a combination of various types of bog plants, the garden can become a new dimension of green blades, arrowheads, or swords. Each bog foliage is shaped differently with flowers of varying colors and sizes.

Little Maintenance

Once constructed and planted, bog gardens require little care, other than occasionally flooding the garden with water.

Wading pools or old bathtubs, lined with PVC, make excellent self-contained receptacles for bog plants whose roots require constant moisture; however, by nature of their growth patterns, bog gardens should be shallow, with only 3- to 6-inches of water.

To build your bog garden, excavate the soil in the chosen garden area to a depth of 12-inches and lay PVC sheeting. (PVC lining helps retain the water and maintains the marshy condition required by bog plants.) Cover the PVC with soil to a depth of 6-inches.

Bog plants are grown in or near the water in mediums ranging from damp soil to 6-inches of water above the soil line. Simply press the roots into submerged or saturated heavy garden soil. To anchor the plants, sheets of wire mesh can be embedded in the soil for plant stability.

The most practical and aesthetic method of using bogs is to plant both deciduous and evergreen types. If planted close together, it is less noticeable when the deciduous plants annually die back. Flood the garden as often as needed during the growing season.

INDOOR PONDS

Although aesthetically beautiful for indoor design, unless constructed properly, indoor water gardens may be difficult to maintain. Water lilies must be rotated indoors and out in order for them to grow, and chemicals are usually required for proper maintenance of the indoor pond.

Before constructing your indoor water garden, take into consideration the following factors:

Plumbing

Large, adequate, accessible plumbing is necessary for proper maintenance of the indoor water garden. A large, 6-inch drain allows the pond to drain easily without clogging. An outside valve that is easily accessible to the drain will also be necessary for efficient pond cleaning.

Splashing

One consideration with the indoor waterfall and/or fountain is splashing. During construction, make certain you allow sufficient area around the fountainhead and the base of the waterfall for splashing. Some types of chemicals soften the water and cut down on the splash, and a custom-made screen covering the top will also cut down on the splashing.

Depth

Indoor ponds should be 18-inches deep for optimum conditions for both fish and plants.

Color

Dark-colored ponds enhance the overall effect of the indoor pond, giving depth and perception, accenting underwater lighting, and hiding any spots on the pond.

Lighting

Full-spectrum, fluorescent lighting is usually the best, particularly for fish. However, placement of this type of lighting is important since it may fade the colors in furniture, carpets and even pictures.

Chemicals

Chemicals for indoor ponds are highly specialized. Check with a water garden supplier for the correct type for your pond, depending on whether or not you have both fish and/or plants.

Overflow

An overflow sytem is not only the easiest method for handling filtration on an indoor pond, but it can also enhance the overall appearance by skimming the surface.

Expert Advice

The necessity for expert advice on construction and maintenance is probably more crucial for the indoor pond than for any other type of water gardening. The fee spent for an expert's advice can save monetary loss and heartache in the future.

CHAPTER 11

History of Water Gardening

HISTORY

Valley of the Temples, Oahu, Hawaii.   *Photo by Dennis Tannen.*

> "Go back with me to the fourth dynasty in Ancient Egypt and see Meten, high priest and powerful official, strolling around his great villa...He watches the ducks and water fowl that float on his ponds rise and resettle among the lotuses of the Nile, and he sighs with contentment that the gods are kind to him. Here at Meten's villa, over three thousand years ago, was the first water garden known to history."
>
> *The Country Home Magazine*
> July, 1931

Yes, enjoyment of water in the garden and aquatic plants dates back through the centuries. Archeological diggings have uncovered evidence showing that the shores of the Nile were planted with aquatic plants. Tomb paintings and representations of lotus and papyrus have been found in ancient temples and tombs. Petals of lotuses and water lilies were found buried with Rameses II and in the wreaths of Amenhotep I.

Water lilies and lotuses also left their images on designs in other countries around the world, from the design of the Ionic capital to etchings on jewelry and idols. The cornucopia, an ancient universal symbol of ferility and abundance, is believed to have been designed from the large seed pod of *nymphaea* lotus, while a Hindu myth of creation tells about Brahma re-creating the universe from the lotus.

The Europeans and English have maintained an affinity for water gardening through the centuries. Ancient water fountains and wells not only served utilitarian purposes, but they adorned many of the public squares and private gardens. Some of the famous European fountains include the Fontana Maggiore in Perugia, Schone Bunnen in Nuremberg, Trevi Fountain in Rome, and the Fountain des Innocents in Paris.

The English have always considered water gardening an integral part of their garden designs, maybe, as some horti-culturists suggest, because they are blessed with considerable rainfall. One of the earliest and best known English water gardens was found at the home of the Duke of Devonshire. In fact, it was Joseph Paxton, gardener to the Duke of Devonshire, who in 1849 revolutionized the design of the greenhouse in order to successfully grow the gigantic *Victoria amazonica*.

Probably the most famous water garden of all times is the beautiful lily pond created by Impressionist artist, Claude Monet, on his four-acre property in Giverny, France. Monet immortalized his water lilies in a series of paintings, *Decoration des Nympheas,* exhibited in the Orangerie Museum in Paris. Today, his garden and cottage, located 50 miles northwest of Paris, have been restored. One of the tour features includes a walk through Monet's large studio which was especially constructed so he could work on his mammoth water lily canvases.

Although water lilies are indigenous to practically every country in the world – Europe, England, United States, Australia, India, Africa, Central and South America, Canada, Indies, Japan, and Siberia, the recognition of these beautiful aquatic flowers in the modern world can probably be directly attributed to the discovery of the gigantic *Victoria amazonica* in 1801 by European botanist Thaddaeus Haenke.

The unusual looking *Victoria amazonica,* native to South America, was discovered by several travelers in the early 1800s. However, it was generally over-looked until 1846 when Thomas Bridges brought the seeds to English gardens. British botanist John Lindley described this plant and named it for Queen Victoria.

In America the first *Victoria amazonica* seeds were grown in Philadelphia, and not long afterwards Longwood Gardens in Pennsylvania developed a spectacular American version by crossbreeding *Victoria amazonica* with the closely related *Victoria cruziana.* In 1853 John Fick Allen exhibited a leaf and flower from the plant to the Massachusetts Horticultural Society. According to William Tricker in *The Water Garden,* 1897, "The introduction of that plant [v. amozonica], as well as of several species of *nymphaea,* into the public parks and gardens became general through the United States."

Thus began the resurgence of interest in water gardening, an interest that grows even today, particularly as technology continues to improve aquatic materials and the plants become hardier.

By no means have public water gardens remained non-existent in the United States. Three of the nation's well known public water gardens include the Kenilworth Aquatic Gardens in Washington D.C., the Longwood Gardens in Kennett Square, Pennsylvania, and the Missouri Botanical Gardens in St. Louis.

Kenilworth Aquatic Gardens,

Washington D. C., at one time the nation's largest commercial water gardening supplier, is today the only national park raising water lilies. The beginnings of the Kenilworth Aquatic Gardens date back to 1882 when Walter B. Shaw transported water lilies from his native state Maine and planted them on his property along the Anacostia River in the District of Columbia. Over the years, he continued to plant and develop some 44 ponds filled with water lilies, lotuses, and a variety of other aquatic plants. In 1912 Shaw's daughter, Helen Fowler, took over the gardens, managing them until 1938 when they were purchased by the East National Capital Parks system.

In 1957 George H. Pring, one of America's finest experts on water gardening, created Longwood Gardens, a 13-pond public garden in Kennett Square, Pennsylvania. The Longwood ponds exhibit collections of both hardy and tropical water lilies.

The beautiful, internationally-famous, 79-acre Missouri Botanical Garden in St. Louis was donated to the city in 1899 by Henry Shaw. After traveling in the United States, Europe and Great Britain, Shaw brought back his many ideas and developed

New Otani Hotel, Tokyo, Japan.   Photo by Carolyn Uber.
Santa Barbara Mission, Santa Barbara, California.
Photo by Carolyn Uber.

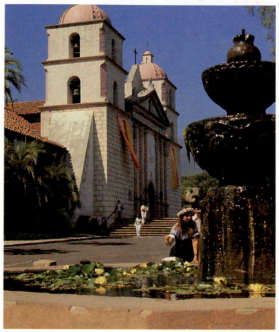

The Cascades Hotel, South Africa.   *Photo courtesy of Lifescapes, Inc.*

one of the world's most famous botanic gardens.

In addition to some of the people already mentioned, many others have made contributions to the history of water gardening – too many, in fact, to mention them all.

Joseph Latour-Marliac – From 1880 to 1937, Joseph Latour-Marliac hybridized hardy water lilies and introduced new, brightly-colored varieties into a water lily world dominated by white, pale pink and pale yellow varieties. Many of Marliac's colorful water lilies were found in Monet's garden pond which served as the inspiration for his famous paintings.

George Pring – The superintendent of the Missouri Botanical Gardens for 63 years, Pring patented the first American hybrid, *St. Louis.* Other contributions in the field of hybridizing include bringing tropical water lilies into their own prominence, developing a smaller lily for average-size ponds, and producing easy-to-cultivate yellow and white water lilies.

William Tricker – A former gardener at London's Kew Gardens, William Tricker opened one of the first water lily nurseries in America in 1895 and introduced his tropical hybrids. He is considered one of the nation's first experts and writers on water gardening. His company, William Tricker, Inc., remains open today, the oldest supplier of aquatics in the world.

G. L. Thomas – In 1917, businessman Leicester Thomas planted a few water lilies in a pool by the roadside of his property in Maryland which began attracting the interest of passerbys. What started as one pond soon expanded into 500 ponds covering 275-acres. Today, Lilypons Water Gardens is one of the nation's largest aquatic suppliers.

Martin Randig – For 35 years Martin Randig quietly went about hybridizing water lilies and keeping detailed records on each cross-pollination. Randig's horticulture experiments in new colors and shades in water lilies have been recognized around the world and in all the major botanical gardens. In fact, many of his colorful hybrids have gained in popularity since his death in 1969.

Ted Uber – Formerly a school teacher, Ted Uber and his wife, Louella, purchased Van Ness Water Gardens in Upland, California in 1952. Not only has Van Ness Water Gardens introduced many new water lilies over the years, including Martin Randig's hybrids, but they have been pioneers in the field of aquatic fertilizers and algaecides. Today, Van Ness Water Gardens is owned and managed by Uber's son, William, who revolutionized aquatic mail order catalogs by offering a 54-page, colorfully-illustrated booklet filled with information covering all facets of water gardening.

Perry D. Slocum – Perry Slocum, a longtime water lily hobbyist, started Slocum Water Gardens in 1938 on the family farm. After making several location changes, the business was relocated on 9-1/2 acres in Florida in 1963, where it is still operated today by Slocum's son, Peter. Although retired, Perry Slocum continues to hybridize and patent his lotuses and hardy water lilies.

John A. Wood – What started as a hobby for hybridizer Jack Wood in 1960 turned into a full time job in the water lily business. Today, Wood and his wife, Janice, singlehandedly operate one of the nation's largest wholesale water lily supply businesses. Wood continues to hybridize and introduce new tropicals to the industry. Three of his well known introductions include *Jack Wood, Janice C. Wood* and *Wood's White Night.*

'Wood's White Knight'.   *Photo by Clint Bryant.*

HISTORY

INDEX

INDEX

INDEX

INDEX